*The American
Immigration Collection*

The Poles
in
America

PAUL FOX

Arno Press and The New York Times

NEW YORK 1970

Reprint Edition 1970 by Arno Press Inc.

LC# 70-129397
ISBN 0-405-00551-2

The American Immigration Collection—Series II
ISBN for complete set 0-405-00543-1

Manufactured in the United States of America

THE POLES
IN AMERICA

PAUL FOX

THE POLES
IN AMERICA

BY

PAUL FOX

PASTOR, ST. PAUL'S PRESBYTERIAN CHURCH, BALTIMORE, MD.

WITH AN INTRODUCTION BY

CHARLES HATCH SEARS

NEW YORK
GEORGE H. DORAN COMPANY

INTRODUCTION

The New Americans Series consists of studies of the following racial groups together with a study of the Eastern Orthodox churches:

Albanian and Bulgarian, Armenian and Assyrian-Chaldean, Czecho-Slovak, Greek, Italian, Jewish, Jugo-Slav (Croatian, Servian, Slovenian), Magyar, Polish, Russian and Ruthenian, or Ukrainian, Spanish (Spaniards) and Portuguese, Syrian.

These studies, made under the auspices of the Interchurch World Movement, were undertaken to show, in brief outline the social, economic and religious background, European or Asiatic, of each group and to present the experience—social, economic and religious—of the particular group in America, with special reference to the contact of the given people with religious institutions in America.

It was designed that the studies should be sympathetic but critical.

It is confidently believed that this series will help America to appreciate and appropriate the spiritual wealth represented by the vast body of New Americans, each group having its own peculiar heritage and potentialities; and will lead Christian America, so far as she will lead them, to become a better lover of mankind.

The writer in each case is a kinsman or has had direct and intimate relationship with the people, or group of peoples, presented. First hand knowledge and the ability to study and write from a deeply sympathetic and broadly Christian viewpoint were primary conditions in the selection of the authors.

The author of this volume was born of Polish parents in Kojkowitz, Austrian Silesia. His preparatory education was obtained in the Imperial Gymnasium in Teschen. After two years in Marietta College, he entered Western Reserve University, from which he received the A.B. and A.M. degrees. He has had four years of post graduate work in Johns Hopkins University. He is also a graduate of Oberlin Theological Seminary. His birth, education and pastoral experience in Polish churches peculiarly fit him to write this Study.

These manuscripts are published through the courtesy of the Interchurch World Movement with the coöperative aid of various denominational boards, through the Home Missions Council of America.

At this writing arrangements have been made for the publication of only six of the series, namely, Czecho-Slovak, Greek, Italian, Pole, Magyar and Russian, but other manuscripts will be published as soon as funds or advanced orders are secured.

A patient review of all manuscripts, together with a checking up of facts and figures, has been made by the Associate Editor, Dr. Frederic A. Gould, to whom we are largely indebted for statistical and verbal accuracy. The editor is responsible for the general plan and scope of the studies and for questions of policy in the execution of this work.

CHARLES HATCH SEARS.

CONTENTS

CONTENTS

ILLUSTRATIONS

CHAPTER I: EUROPEAN BACKGROUND

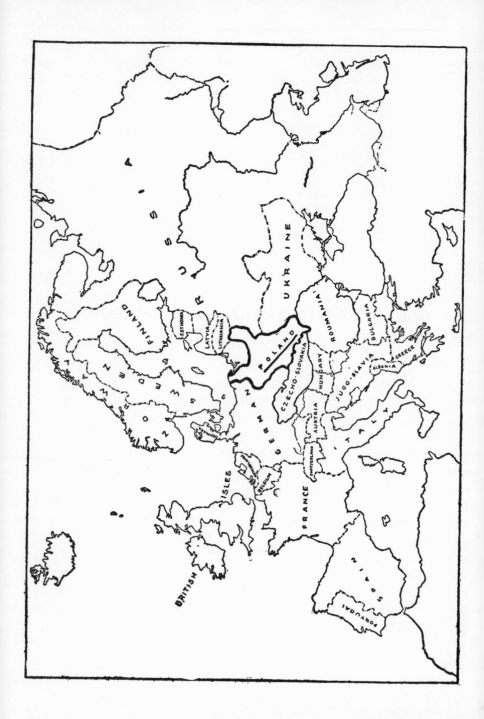

THE POLES IN AMERICA

Chapter I

EUROPEAN BACKGROUND

HISTORICAL DEVELOPMENT

Introductory

Racial classification and early home.—The Poles
are Slavs. They form the westernmost branch of
the Slavic race. Their home, since prehistoric
times, has been Central Europe, the region east and
west of the Vistula River between the Baltic Sea
and the Carpathian Mountains.

Influence of location on national development.—
Owing to this central location, the Poles came very
early into contact with both civilizations, eastern
and western, and as a result developed rapidly economically, culturally, and politically. So remarkable was this development that the English historian Bain says: "In the middle of the sixteenth
century Poland bore upon her the full promise of
Empire. . . . She was indisputably the greatest
power of central Europe, and the whole world regarded her as the chief representative of the
Slavonic race." [1] And the famous German general
C. von Moltke, who certainly cannot be suspected of
Polish partisanship, in his "Historical Sketch of
Poland," published in London in 1895, stated that

[1] Bain, The Last King of Poland, p. 1.

Poland prior to her partitions was "the most civilized country in Europe." [2]

Divisions of Polish history.—Polish history naturally divides itself into five periods, namely: I. The Formative Period of Polish National Life (960-1306); II. The Period of Growing Power, Prosperity, and Influence (1306-1586); III. The Period of Decline and Final Fall (1587-1795); IV. The Period of Subjugation and of National Struggle for Independence (1795-1918); and V. The Restoration (1918-). The first is the period of the formation of monarchical power under the rule of the Piast dynasty (960-1384). The second period marks a transition from a monarchy to a republic of nobles under the Jagiellos (1386-1572). The third is the period of elective kings (1572-1795) and is characterized by reaction and disorganization, by a decline in power and in influence. The fourth is the period of repeated attempts on the part of the Poles to regain their independence. And the fifth —the period of Poland's reëstablishment as an independent nation as a result of the World War.

I: The Formative Period of Polish National Life, 960-1306.

Poland's historical beginning.—The Polish State emerges upon the scene of history with the consolidation of the Polish tribes under Mieszko I (960-992), and with the introduction of Christianity into Poland through Mieszko's marriage to the Bohemian princess Dubravka, both of which events marked the beginning of a successful resistance of the Poles to Teutonic aggression, conquest, and to their policy of extermination under the cover of Christianization of the heathen Slavs.

[2] Quoted by Dr. Radosavlejevich in his Who Are the Slavs? Vol. I, p. 82.

Christianity's influence on economic development.
—The introduction of Christianity not only saved
the Poles from further exterminative conquests by
the Germans and gave them a new religion, but also
brought about an improvement in their economic
conditions. The monastic Orders taught the Poles
the use of improved agricultural implements, and
showed them how to reclaim swampy lands by
drainage, build better and more comfortable houses,
plant orchards, and do many other things they had
not known before. They also gave an impetus to
the development of industry by bringing with them
skilled craftsmen to produce certain necessary
things which the natives did not know how to make.[3]

**Poland's ecclesiastical and political independence
of the German Empire under Boleslaw the Brave,
992-1025.**—Under Mieszko I's successor, Boleslaw
the Brave (992-1025), by the incorporation of neighboring Slavic tribes, Poland gained greatly in territory, and asserted both its ecclesiastical and its political independence of the German Empire; the
first by the establishment of an archbishopric at
Gniezno in 1000 A. D., and the second by the coronation of Boleslaw as King of Poland in 1025 by the
archbishop of Poland "in the presence of Boleslaw's
feudatories and his great army of twenty thousand
warriors."[4]

Three centuries of reverses.—After Boleslaw's
death in 1025 the young, rapidly developed kingdom
was forced to undergo a period of nearly three centuries of repeated reverses—a trial so severe that
it was sufficient to disrupt for good any ordinary
body politic.

(a) **Wars with jealous neighbors.**—First came a
series of wars with jealous neighbors, the German
Empire, Bohemia, Hungary, the Duchy of Kiev, and

---

[3] Cf. Dr. E. H. Lewinski-Corwin, Pol. Hist. of Poland, p. 14.
[4] Ibidem, p. 21.

Denmark. Taking advantage of Mieszko II's (1025-1034) inertia and lack of foresight and daring, these jealous enterprising neighbors decided to compensate themselves for their territorial losses during Boleslaw's reign; Germany took Lusatia; Bohemia, Moravia; Hungary, Slovakia; the Duchy of Kiev, Red Russia, or eastern Galicia; and Denmark, Pomerania. Poland was thus stripped of nearly all her territorial acquisitions under Boleslaw the Brave.

(b) Internal political and religious reaction and consequent disorganization.—Next followed a savage reaction against the growing burdensome power of the State and particularly against the exploitation of the Church. With the growth of the power of the State the earlier patriarchal form of government was gradually displaced by a more centralized administration, curtailing the people's liberty and at the same time imposing heavier burdens upon them in the form of taxes. For to preserve the territorial unity of the State the king was compelled to maintain a large standing army, the support of which could be secured only through increased taxation. A more centralized administration required a growing official class and greater Court splendor, the maintenance of which had to fall also upon the State treasury. Moreover, the imposition upon the people of tithes for the support of the Church and the clergy, mostly foreign and hated, made that burden all the heavier and more obnoxious. As a result of this oppressive taxation by Church and State and the harsh treatment experienced at the hands of feudal lords and the clergy, the people rose in revolt, burned and demolished cities, castles, churches and monasteries, in many places murdered the hated priests and monks, and reverted to paganism.[5]

[5] Cf. Dr. Lewinski-Corwin, pp. 15-22.

(c) Struggle for supremacy among the princes resulting in weakness of monarchical power.—Reorganization of the administration and partial reconquest of lost territory brought in a period of restored order and of renewed strength. This, however, did not last long. It was soon followed by a period of bitter struggle among the members of the princely family for supremacy in the State. It resulted from Boleslaw III's (1102-1138) division of the principality of Poland among his surviving sons with the establishment of the principle of seniority. This made the sons independent rulers of their respective provinces. The oldest, however, was to receive the Duchy of Cracow in addition to his hereditary province, and, as the Grand Duke of Cracow, was to be the supreme head of the whole State of Poland. The arrangement suited the aristocracy and the clergy, who disliked a strong centralized government, excellently well. But it led to ceaseless civil strife, and marked the beginning of the decline of monarchical power in Poland. For, as Dr. Lewinski-Corwin says, "the authority of the Duke of Cracow was not adequately defined by law and was nil in practice. The heads of the smaller principalities were, in fact, independent rulers. They were free to establish alliances for defensive and offensive warfare, to make treaties, and to maintain independent customs-barriers. In other words, Poland of the thirteenth century was no longer one solid political entity. The sovereignty of the former state became diffused among a number of smaller independent political units, with only the common bonds of language, race, religion, and tradition." [6]

Its advantages to the aristocracy and the clergy.—This state of political affairs was greatly in the interest of the aristocracy and of the clergy. These two classes acquired large land holdings with juris-

[6] Political Hist. of Poland, pp. 31-34.

diction over their peasants, and became very powerful in the thirteenth century. The Church, in particular, grew stronger steadily due to its splendid organization, its genius for accumulation of wealth, its moral control over the people, its greater independence resulting from the adoption in Poland of the Gregorian reforms, and to its representation in the Prince's Council since 1180 A. D. Thus with the growing weakness of the monarchical power increased the wealth, strength, and influence of the two specially privileged classes, the barons and the clergy; and consequently both classes were putting forth every effort to maintain the existing disorder of things.

(d) **Tartar invasions.**—Besides these troubles, Poland suffered much from the Tartars and from the Teutonic Knights. In 1241 savage hordes of Tartars from Asia invaded Poland, and ruthlessly plundered, pillaged, devastated, and depopulated the country. After they had laid the country waste completely, their attack broke at last on the field of Lignica, in Silesia, before the Polish cavalry, which arrested their further invasion of Europe, and thereby saved Western civilization.[7] The Tartars flowed back into the steppes of the Volga, whence from time to time they sent plundering expeditions into Poland; but never again succeeded in conquering her, nor even in passing through her territories in order to plunder and lay waste other countries. Poland, says Drogoslaw, "thus became the true rampart of the West and of Western civilization for many centuries, and shed streams of her blood in holding back first the Tartar hordes and later the Turkish armies, which menaced the very existence of the civilized world. It is impossible to say what might have become of the western peoples and the

[7] Drogoslaw, Poland, p. 3; Dufour, Petite Histoire de Pologne, p. 9.

whole civilization of Central Europe if the Polish nation, though politically split into fragments, had not stood its ground, watchful, heroic, always ready to make every sacrifice." [8]

(e) The Teutonic Knights.—The other source of constant trouble was the Order of the Teutonic Knights. Invited to Poland in 1228 by Conrad of Mazovia to protect his territories against frequent incursions of the barbarian Prussians, they, having just been expelled from Hungary by Andrew II on account of their political pretensions, joyfully accepted this new offer, and settled in the district of Culm, roughly corresponding to modern West Prussia, granted them for their quarters by Conrad. These militant Knights, to secure themselves against the possibility of similar expulsion from Poland as had just befallen them in Hungary, put themselves under the protection of the Pope and the German Emperor, procured from both confirmations of Conrad's falsified grant, and then took up the Christianization and subjugation of the Prussians systematically. In the "Christianized" territory, they established German colonies, built fortresses, and organized a powerful State. Having established themselves in conquered Prussia, and confident in the protection of the Pope and the German Emperor, they turned against Poland, shut her off from the sea, and became her most bitter and troublesome enemy until they were at last completely subdued by Casimir IV in 1466.

The end of Poland's "Dark Ages."—The close of the thirteenth century marked the end of Poland's "Dark Ages" of external aggressions, internal disorders, political divisions, administrative weakness, and of consequent purgatorial trials and sufferings; the end of a period in which the aristocracy and particularly the Church with its powerful clergy reigned

[8] Poland, p. 3.

supreme, and the princes were their humble dependent vassals.

II: The Period of Growing Power, Prosperity, and Influence, 1306-1586.

The dawn of a new era.—The beginning of the fourteenth century ushered in the dawn of a new era. The next three centuries were centuries of growth and progress; of internal reorganization, external expansion, and of ever-increasing political power and prestige.

The significance of the fourteenth century.—The fourteenth century witnessed the unification of the different Polish provinces, the reëstablishment of royal power and authority together with the restoration of the royal title lost in the eleventh century, the re-conquest of territories taken from Poland in time of her disunion and weakness, the reorganization and development of the nation along administrative, judicial, educational, and economic lines, the beginning of a new dynasty, and the voluntary union of Lithuania with Poland in 1386.

Restoration of Poland's power under Wladyslaw I, 1306-1333.—The unification of the Polish provinces and the recovery of the royal title was successfully effected with the aid of the Hungarians by Wladyslaw I, the Short, 1306-1333, in spite of the powerful opposition of Brandenburg, the German Emperor, the German element in the city of Cracow, the clergy, Great Poland, and Bohemia. The odds against Wladyslaw were so great and his achievement was so remarkable that he may truly be regarded as the first real restorer of Poland. Having successfully overcome all stubborn opposition, Wladyslaw united Great and Little Poland, and in 1320 was crowned King of Poland at Cracow, which henceforth until the close of the sixteenth century became the capital of united Poland. To secure himself against the jealousy of Germany and Bohemia and their aggressions, he effected a number of skillful foreign alliances; in 1315 with the Scandinavian countries, in 1320 with Hungary, by giving his daughter Elizabeth in marriage to the Hungarian king, Charles Robert, and in 1325 with Lithuania, by securing the hand of Grand Duke Gedymin's daughter, Anna Aldona, for his son Kazimir. Assisted by Emperor Louis of Germany and the Margrave of Brandenburg, John of Luxemburg, King of Bohemia, who as son-in-law of Waclaw I claimed the right to the throne of Poland, made war on Wladyslaw in 1327, but Wladyslaw died in the midst of the struggle in 1333, leaving the settlement of the war to his son and successor, Kazimir, 1333-1370.

Reorganization of the state by Kazimir the Great, 1333-1370.—Kazimir's chief endeavor was to make peace with the enemy, even though it cost Poland the cession to Bohemia of "the pearl of the Polish Crown," the westernmost part of Silesia,—to a part of which, the principality of Teschen, the Czechs lay claim today on fourteenth century historical grounds,—in order that he might devote all his attention and energies to domestic problems, economic, social, administrative, judicial, and educational, the internal reorganization, development, and strengthening of the politically unified nation. His long reign of thirty-seven years made it possible for him to achieve his object. He brought about uniformity in Polish law by the codification of existing laws, reorganized the judicial system of the country, readjusted the relation between the peasantry and the landlords, facilitated colonization, granted special protection to towns and furthered their growth, stimulated industry and commerce through monetary reforms and the improvement of the means of communication, established the

University of Cracow, and encouraged education.
It is of interest and worth while to remember that
the University of Cracow was the second of its kind
in Central Europe, following that of Prague by six-
teen years and preceding the University of Vienna
by one year, of Heidelberg by two years, of Erfurt
by twenty-eight, and that of Leipzig by forty-five
years. In Kazimir's time Poland had a number of
eminent writers, scientists, and jurists. In the development of the cities and in the growth of their
wealth and importance Kazimir saw a support of
the kingly power against the disquietingly growing
might and lawlessness of the magnates and nobility
and against the independence of the Church.[9]

By the end of Kazimir's reign Poland was unified
politically, not only in the person of the king, as
in Wladyslaw's case, but through the legal, economic, and social reforms Kazimir had been able to
bring about. As his father had been the restorer of
Poland's external political unity, so Kazimir was
the restorer of Poland's internal unity, prosperity,
and strength.

Territorial expansion under Kazimir the Great.
—Moreover, besides his beneficent internal reforms,
Kazimir extended Poland's boundaries eastward by
reincorporating definitely into Poland, Red Russia,
with its capital of Lwow, or what we now know as
eastern Galicia.

**The beginning of a new dynasty: The Jagiellos,
1386-1572. Union of Lithuania with Poland.**—With
the death of Kazimir the Great in 1370 the Piast
dynasty of Polish rulers came to an end. The Polish
crown passed over by agreement and on certain conditions [10] to Kazimir's nephew, Louis of Hungary,
and finally to his younger daughter Jadwiga, who
was given away in marriage by the Polish nobility

[9] See Dr. Lewinski-Corwin, p. 62.
[10] Ibidem, pp. 64-65.

to Jagiello, Grand Duke of Lithuania, in 1386, and in that way a union of Lithuania with Poland was effected in the person of the king,—a union which later on was voluntarily confirmed by the pact of Horodlo, 1413, and made indissoluble by the pact of Lublin of 1569.

The significance of the fifteenth century. The Renaissance in Poland.—The fifteenth century in Polish history was marked by the introduction of the Renaissance into Poland, the spread of the Hussite Movement, the supremacy of the State over the Church, Poland's conquest of the Teutonic Knights, and by the growth of the power of the gentry.

In 1400 King Wladyslaw Jagiello generously endowed the University of Cracow, reorganized and enlarged it by adding to the departments of law, medicine, and philosophy, the department of theology. Soon the fame of the reorganized university spread all over Europe, the university became a center of humanistic learning, attracted the scholastic world of western Europe, and counted among its graduates a great number of learned men. In its faculty it had such distinguished men as Adalbert Brudziew, mathematician and astronomer, teacher of Copernicus, and Matthew Miechow, distinguished for his medical knowledge and works. The enrollment of the university was very large, and both the students and the faculty were drawn from all classes of society and from many countries. In the second half of the fifteenth century nearly half of the students enrolled were of foreign birth.[11] The university became a living link connecting Poland with European education and science.[12] As early as 1416 the University of Cracow acquired a European reputation

---

[11] See Dr. Lewinski-Corwin, p. 73; Litwinski, Intellectual Poland, p. 32.
[12] Prof. Tarnowski, quoted by Dr. Corwin, p. 75.

so far as to venture upon forwarding an expression
of its views in connection with the deliberations of
the Council of Constance, siding with the French
theologians in support of the supremacy of Church
Councils over the Papacy,[13] and toward the close
of the fifteenth century it was in high repute as
a school of both astronomical and humanistic
studies.[14]

Among the distinguished scholars and writers of
this century were George of Sanok, who contributed
a great deal toward the awakening of interest in the
ancient authors and in their philosophy of life; John
Ostrorog (1420-1501), who wrote a remarkable
treatise advocating the subordination of the Church
to the State; Paul of Brudziew, rector of the University of Cracow and author of the "Tractatus de
potestate Papæ et Imperatoris respectu Infidelium,"
presented to the Council of Constance in 1415; and
foremost among them all the historian John Dlugosz
(1415-1480), author of "the most profound historical
works of the fifteenth century. The erudition of
the author, the painstaking examination of the
sources, his searching criticism and gift of analysis
and observation, his masterful classification and
method of presentation marked an era in history
writing and laid solid foundations for all future national histories of Poland." [15]

The Hussite movement.—Another thing that pro-
foundly stirred the life of the Polish nation in the
fifteenth century was the Hussite movement. It
spread to Poland early, and won many adherents
and sympathizers. The Hussites of Bohemia had
gone so far as to offer the crown of their country
to the Jagiellos. The offer was not accepted due to
the powerful influence of Cardinal Zbigniew Oleś-

[13] Prof. Alex. Bruckner, Hist. Lit. Polskiej, I, p. 26.
[14] Enc. Brit., 1911, XXVII, p. 757.
[15] Dr. Lewinski-Corwin, p. 104.

nicki and the strong reactionary clerical party in Poland. The Hussite movement, however, as it spread through the country, created a new religious atmosphere, and prepared the way to the emancipation of the State from the domination of the Church by King Kazimir IV (1447-1492) and for the reformation of the sixteenth century.

The Supremacy of the State over the Church in Poland.—Kazimir's first step after the coronation was to restrict the power of the clergy by subordinating the Church to the State. In this he was aided materially by two circumstances—the then existing strife between the Polish gentry and the Polish clergy over the payment of tithes (the gentry insisting upon paying them in specie, and the clergy upon payments in kind), and the schism in the Church which resulted from the controversy regarding the superiority of Church Councils over the Popes. In the long-drawn-out struggle the king won; the nomination of bishops, or the right of investiture lost in the thirteenth century to the Church, became henceforth a recognized attribute of the Polish kings.

Defeat of the Teutonic Knights: Poland at the height of European power.—Then, too, in the fifteenth century, by defeating the Teutonic Knights Poland attained great importance as a European power. Poland's victory over the Knights in the battle of Grunwald in 1410 broke the power of the Order, and put an end to German domination over Polish lands. In 1466 Jagiello's younger son, Kazimir IV (1447-1492), crushed the Knights completely and definitely, and forced them by the Peace of Thorn, of the same year, to restore to Poland the territories formerly torn from her, namely West Prussia, Ermland, and the eastern part of Pomerania, including the city of Gdańsk, or Danzig. Thus Poland regained access to the Baltic, and was now again enabled to communicate freely with the outside world. Unfortunately, however, it made a serious mistake in that it had not driven out the Teutonic Knights altogether from the territories in which they had established themselves; and in that it had allowed (1525) Albert of Hohenzollern, the Grand Master of the Order, to become the secular prince of the vassal province of East Prussia, even though the Dukes of Prussia promised to recognize Poland's sovereignty, and agreed to pay homage and tribute to the Polish king. This concession led to a gradual Germanization of the Polish population of East Prussia and to the transformation of the vassal duchy into a powerful German state, which was destined to play such a sinister part in the history of Poland and of Europe.[16]

Growing power of the "szlachta."—The fifteenth century marked also the growth of the power of the Polish nobility, or *szlachta*. As the *szlachta* paid with its blood for victories on innumerable battle-fields, it held that these sacrifices were worthy of reward in the form of special privileges and liberties not enjoyed by other classes. The extinction of the Piast dynasty in 1370 afforded it the first opportunity for the exaction of special privileges for itself as a class. The throne of Poland made vacant by the death of Kazimir the Great, fell to Kazimir's nephew, Louis of Anjou, King of Hungary. Louis, however, having no male issue and desiring to secure the crown for one of his daughters, accorded the Polish nobility by the Pact of Koszyce, in Hungary, 1374, privileges which made their class more powerful to the detriment of the royal authority. During the succeeding century these privileges grew steadily until at the close of the fifteenth century we see the Polish nobility at the helm of government.

The origin of the "Sejm."—With the accession

[16] Cf. Dr. Lewinski-Corwin, pp. 131-133.

to the throne of Poland of John I Olbracht (1492-1501) the Polish "Sejm," or National Diet, comes into being, and from now on to the end Poland has a regular parliamentary government, in which the nobility, particularly the knighthood or gentry, plays the leading rôle. Thus the power of the king, which in western Europe developed on the ruins of feudalism, and ultimately in consequence of religious strife grew absolute, became limited in Poland, and in 1501 the rôle of the Polish king was reduced to that of the President of the Senate.

Its composition, privileges, and powers.—The National Diet consisted of two chambers, the Senate, composed of lay and church dignitaries and the Chamber of Deputies, the members of which were elected by the county diets from among the gentry. As in all parliamentary governments, the Chamber of Deputies was the more powerful and influential; its decisions were determining. Freedom of speech was subject to no restrictions. Inviolability of property and person were guaranteed by law; the first by the pact of 1422, the second by the privilege of 1433. The Polish "Neminem captivabimus nisi jure victum" provision of 1433 preceded the English "Habeas Corpus Act" by two hundred and forty-six years. The szlachta reached the climax of its political aspirations when in 1505 it secured the passage of the statute known as "Nihil novi," providing that nothing new could be done or undertaken by the king without the common consent of both the Senate and the Chamber of Deputies. Thus with the opening of the sixteenth century the "Sejm" became the legislative and most important governmental organ in Poland and the szlachta the most powerful and influential element.

The sixteenth century—the "Golden Age" of Poland's history.—In the sixteenth century Poland reached the climax, not only of its political development, but also of its material prosperity, its literary and artistic glory, and of its international influence. The sixteenth century was the "Golden Age" of Poland's history in every sense of the term.

Economic prosperity of the fifteenth and sixteenth centuries.—In 1466 Prussia, with its seaports, became a part of Poland, and the whole course of the Vistula River returned under the control of the Polish government. This gave a great impetus to commerce and agriculture. Large freight fleets sailed upon the Vistula, carrying cargoes of wheat, rye, hemp, tar, honey, wax, bristles, fats, lumber, skins, and furs to Danzig. The enormous growth of exports produced a marked effect upon the cities. Due to the introduction of credit on an extensive scale, they grew in wealth, and many families acquired great riches. Private mansions, artistic public buildings, and beautiful churches adorned the towns. Art flourished. Wit Stwosz, the great Polish sculptor of the time, was a natural product of his age. Many foreign, particularly Italian, architects were brought over to design public and private buildings. In daily life the burghers wore sumptuous dress of silk and lace, fine furs, gold, jewelry, and precious stones. Poor indeed was the master artisan or merchant who did not use silver table ware at home and whose wife did not possess a bonnet ornamented with pearls. The many gold, silver, and bronze candelabra, chandeliers, candlesticks, and other domestic utensils left from that period, still found in churches, museums, and in private families as heirlooms, bear ample testimony to the prosperity of the Polish cities and of the country at large in the fifteenth and sixteenth centuries.[17]

The spread of the Reformation to Poland.—The Reformation, which spread all over Europe in the sixteenth century, and stirred the life of every na-

[17] See Dr. Lewinski-Corwin, pp. 111-117.

THE WAWEL; CRACOW

THE CHURCH OF ST. MARY: CRACOW

[See page 31

tion to its very foundations, speedily penetrated into Poland, and grew influential rapidly. Lutheranism found favor with the German population of the cities; Calvinism—with the Polish nobility, particularly with the magnates and nobles of Little Poland; Hussitism, revived under the name of the Bohemian Brethren—with the people of Great Poland; and Socinianism, or Unitarianism—with the Ruthenian population of eastern Galicia. Among the native Poles Calvinism was more popular than Lutheranism or any other form of the religious reform movement for the simple reason that it was non-German in origin and that it admitted laymen to church councils, giving them a part in the government of the Church. On that account it was considered as more appropriate for a free state and a free people.[18] So rapid was the growth of the Reformation in Poland that by the middle of the sixteenth century the Protestants were absolutely supreme in the National Diet, and invariably elected a Calvinist as marshal of the Diet. At the Diet of 1555 they boldly demanded a national synod, absolute toleration, and the equalization of all sects, except the Antitrinitarians.[19] And so powerful was the influence of the Reformation on the intellectual and spiritual life of the nation that the sixteenth century is known in Polish history as the ''Golden Age'' of Polish culture and literature.

The development of literature and the fine arts.— With prosperity came the fine arts. Science, art, and literature flourished, and Polish culture reached an unprecedented degree of development. It was the fruit of the Renaissance and the Reformation as well as Polish freedom and tolerance. Owing to the somewhat reactionary policy of the University of Cracow at this time, the Polish nobility and the

[18] See Dr. Lewinski-Corwin, p. 139.
[19] Enc. Brit., Art. ''Poland.'' Bain, Slavonic Europe, pp. 77-78.

burgesses sent their sons abroad, to the universities
of Germany, Italy, and France. The young men returned with new ideas about life, government, and
religion, and full of enthusiasm over them and of
zeal in their propagation. The popularity of the
Reformation at home still further augmented this
enthusiasm and zeal. A host of talented writers
appeared. Some discussed matters of state freely,
and criticized the existing conditions, pointing out,
as did the highly gifted Andrew Frycz Modrzewski,
the necessity of equalization of all the estates before
the law, and the advantages of a prosperous free
peasantry. Others, like Orzechowski, thundered
against the despotism of the nobility, the iniquities
and the foreign character of the Church, and the
great privileges of the Jews in matters of money
lending and usury. Historians, poets, dramatists,
and fiction writers sprang up in large numbers
among all classes of society.[20]

**The influence of the Reformation on Polish lan-
guage and literature.**—With the spread of the Reformation the Polish language came into use in literature, displacing Latin. The Bible was translated
into Polish, and a large number of pamphlets intended for the mass of the people was written in
Polish. In 1536 even the City Council of Cracow
proclaimed Polish as the language to be used in
prayers and sermons in the churches of the city.
German and Latin books began to give way to Polish prints.

Polish literature had its beginning with Nicholas
Rey (1505-1569), a Protestant, an ardent advocate
of Calvinism in Poland, an eminent writer and
wholesome philosopher, and the greatest satirist of
the time. His pictures of life, men, manners, and
customs of the time are masterpieces of style, wit,
and clearness of expression, and served as models

[20] Dr. Lewinski-Corwin, p. 146.

to many succeeding writers. Another vigorous, incisive, and voluminous writer in Latin and Polish was Stanislaw Orzechowski (1613-1566). He was a relative of Rey, and for a time a very bitter opponent of the Roman Catholic Church, but a man without stable principles. Andrew Frycz Modrzewski (1503-1572) wrote a great deal, but largely in Latin, and was a fearless champion of reforms in State and Church. He was a friend of Melancthon and a life-long supporter of the Reformation. Martin Bielski (1495-1575), a Protestant, wrote a history of Poland in Polish. The greatest literary figure of this age, however, was Jan Kochanowski (1530-1584). In his poetical writings he displayed great mastery of the Polish language. His poems and dramas delight the most fastidious taste by their beauty, deep thought, and fine sentiment, and are considered as a model of highly cultured language to the present time. Kochanowski was a true son of the Renaissance, indifferent to the Church of Rome though devout, imbued with republican ideas, broad- and liberal-minded.[21] Some of the most beautiful religious songs to this day are from his pen. The stimulus given to writing in Polish supplied by the religious reformers gained momentum as time advanced, and as early as 1548, at the funeral of King Sigismund I, the Old, the Bishop of Cracow, for the first time in history, used Polish on so solemn an occasion.[22]

Thus, in the sixteenth century, Poland reached the zenith of its territorial expansion, its political greatness and influence, its economic prosperity, its parliamentary government, its culture and its religious life and tolerance.

[21] Jan Holewinski, Hist. of Polish Literature, p. 187.
[22] Dr. Lewinski, p. 149.

III: The Period of Decline and Fall, 1587-1795.

Poland's decline: its causes.—The seventeenth and eighteenth centuries were centuries of decay, decline, and final fall of Poland. The causes of this decline and final fall were various, and in their deteriorating effect upon the life of the nation and the body politic—cumulative.

(a) The elective kingship.—First, there was the elective kingship with all its attendant mischievous consequences, political bargaining, bribery, foreign interferences, lack of interest on the part of the sovereigns in Poland's welfare due to their limited tenure of office, and frequent interregna with unsettled conditions resulting from them.

(b) The Catholic reaction.—Then, there was the Catholic reaction, stemming the tide of intellectual and religious progress, fomenting dissensions, spreading intolerance and persecutions, getting control of education and setting back the clock of Poland's intellectual and spiritual progress by two to three centuries.

(c) Outside interference.—Next, came constant outside interference in Poland's internal affairs in an effort to maintain the existing disorder of things in order to profit by it. Russia, Prussia, and Austria did all they could to make it impossible for the Poles to set their house in order, and then charged the Poles with inability to govern themselves, and used that as a pretext for the partition of Poland.

(d) The blind selfishness of the aristocracy.—And, as a strong reënforcement of the cause just described, there was the blind, egotistic selfishness and greed of the aristocracy, which led them, in their desire to build up their private fortunes, whether material or political, into the trap of foreign false promises and entangling alliances, and thus to an unwitting betrayal and sacrifice of their country.

Poland's fall: the partitions.—Suffering from these and other ills, the country could not forever resist their deteriorating and destructive effects as well as the growing aggressiveness and territorial greed of her neighbors. In the end it had to succumb to the inevitable, and her three partitions followed; the first in 1772, the sceond in 1793, and the third in 1795. By these three partitions Russia obtained the lion's share of the prey, Prussia—the next largest, and Austria had to content herself with the smallest portion.

IV: The Period of National Struggle for Independence, 1795-1918.

The partitions made an end of Poland as an independent state; but not of the Polish nation as a living, active, and growing organism, struggling desperately for existence. Poland's political form was torn asunder, but her spiritual life incarnated in the lives of her people continued. It asserted and reasserted its vitality and its virility by repeated insurrections until, in 1914-1918, the power and the importance of the Polish nation became generally felt and recognized, and as a result the nation rose again to new political independence.

V: The Restoration, 1918.

With the reëstablishment of Poland as a new political power, in 1918, Polish history begins a new period—the Restoration. The beginning is very hopeful and very promising. The provisional government is in the hands of sane, far-sighted, moderate progressives, with Marshal Joseph Pilsudski at the head. New Poland is a Republic, and will remain a Republic, with a most liberal democratic constitution. During the three years of its independent political existence the nation has weathered the storm of war that has still raged unabated around it, has successfully coped with all sorts of difficulties, and has, in spite of all odds, made wonderful progress in the reorganization and reconstruction of its political, economic, and social life. As always in its history, so now again Poland is abreast with the times, in the front ranks of progress. It fully recognizes the rights of all social classes, of the peasantry, the industrial class as well as of those enjoying heretofore special privileges and is moving in the direction of a sane solution of pressing economic and social problems fearlessly, but judiciously. It is neither timidly reactionary, nor recklessly radical. It exhibits the wisdom and foresight characteristic of real statesmanship. As to equal rights for men and women, Poland is the one nation that has granted women full suffrage rights without the women having been forced to fight for them. All Poland needs is a fair chance, and it will work out its destiny.

ECONOMIC CONDITIONS OF THE POLISH PEASANTRY

Poland essentially an agricultural country.—Poland is essentially an agricultural country; the great majority of her people derive their subsistence from tilling the soil. Before the war, in Russian Poland, 73.4% of the population were living in villages; in Prussian Poland—69.3%; and in Austrian Poland—80.1%.[23] In other words, before the war in eastern Galicia, for instance, sixty-seven persons in a square kilometer lived by agriculture, in western Galicia—eighty persons, while in the rest of old Austria the figure was thirty-six, and for Germany only thirty-four.[24]

[23] Journal of the Am.-Polish Chamber of Com., Dec., 1920, p. 5.
[24] Dr. A. Górski, Braki krajowej produkcji w Galicji, p. 35.

Economic condition of Polish peasantry, poor. Causes therefor.—The economic condition of the Polish peasantry has unfortunately been very poor and deplorable thus far, owing to (a) small land-holdings, (b) primitive method of agriculture, (c) high taxation, (d) lack of industrial development, and (e) low wages.

(a) **Small landholdings.**—Each peasant owns a strip of land. These peasant holdings vary considerably as to size, and in many, if not in most, instances are inadequate to give their owners sufficient support. In Poznania farms of five hectares,[25] or about twelve acres and less, constitute only 6.8% of the total land-area; in Galicia such farms constitute 84.4%; and in former Russian Poland farms of less than 3.4 hectares constitute 37.1% of the total land-area and farms of less than 8.5 hectares—44.4%.[26] Moreover, these holdings are divided among the children of the household, and this tends to make them smaller with each succeeding generation. In Galicia in 1882 a peasant holding averaged 5 *"morgi,"* [27] or approximately 7 acres, and in 1896 the average dropped down to 4.2 *"morgi,"* or to less than six acres. And it has been estimated that the lowest minimum necessary for the support of a peasant family is 10 *"morgi,"* or about 13 acres.[28]

(b) **Small productiveness.**—To these small peasant holdings, and partly as an inevitable result of them, there is added small productiveness. The productiveness of land on large estates is relatively satisfactory, but that of peasant land is very poor. Galicia, for instance, produced, in 1902-11, 11 quintals [29] of wheat, 12 of barley, and 11 of rye per one

[25] One hectare—2.47 acres.
[26] Journal Am.-Pol. Chamber of Com., for Dec., 1920, p. 5.
[27] One "morg"—1.32 acres.
[28] Dr. L. Caro, Emigracja, p. 77.
[29] One quintal—220.46 pounds.

hectare of land, while Germany produced, in 1908-
12, 20.7 quintals of wheat, 20.1 of barley, and 17.8
of rye per hectare.[30] Galicia, deducting seed, produced before the war 112 kilograms of wheat, rye,
and corn per inhabitant; Russia, deducting exports
and seed, produced 370 kilograms of cereals per inhabitant; Germany, 200; France, of wheat alone,
240, and England about 190. Galicia, therefore,
produced cereals from two to three times less than
she needed for her own consumption according to
western European standards.[31] Neither Galicia, nor
former Russian Poland produced before the war
enough corn to feed their own populations. Galicia,
to be sure, exported some grain, but it imported one-
fourth of the flour it consumed from Hungary, that
is, about two and a half million quintals, or 25,000
carloads. And Russian Poland's annual grain defi-
cit was nearly constant, amounting to about 3,000,-
000 quintals.[32] Only in Prussian Poland did the cultivation of the soil reach a reasonably high
degree of development. The average yield per acre
in this district was twice that of the other districts.[33]

As to live-stock, the kingdom, that is former Russian Poland, furnished the city of Warsaw before
the war only 5% of the total consumption of meat,
the other 95% had to be imported from Russia.
Galicia exported some live-stock, but the export was
gradually diminishing, and consisted chiefly of
pigs.[34]

This small productiveness is the result of primitive agricultural methods, namely, lack of agricultural intelligence, inadequate agricultural tools and

[30] Dr. Górski, p. 33-34.
[31] Ibidem, pp. 34-35.
[32] Ibidem, p. 31.
[33] Journal of Am.-Polish Chamber of Com., Dec., 1920, p. 5.
[34] Dr. Górski, p. 31.

machinery, insufficient fertilization of the soil, and poor agricultural credit facilities. [35]

(c) **High taxation.**—Another cause of the unsatisfactory economic condition of the Polish peasantry has been high taxation. In 1882 the number of those paying land taxes in Galicia was 1,420,020; by 1896 it rose to 1,743,792. This number included 2,978 large land-owners, with estates of 132 acres or more (100 "*morgi*"), and 1,740,814 peasants, with holdings averaging less than six acres (4.2 "*morgi*").[36] And these poor peasants were the ones that had to bear the lion's share of the burden of taxation, national, provincial, and local. The same conditions in respect of taxation prevailed in the other parts of Poland, modified, of course, by local differences.

(d) **Lack of industrial development.**—From the foregoing description of conditions it is evident that the Polish peasant, in order to live at all and at the same time meet his share of the taxes imposed upon him, had to supplement the product of his small farm by outside work. Here, again, the chances to get such work at home were few. The large estates employed a certain number of peasants in the cultivation of their land; but such employment was only seasonal, during harvest time in the summer and during the potato-digging season in the fall. During the long winters the surplus peasant labor had to remain idle; for factories, being few, did not afford much or any opportunity for work. Owing to high taxation, national and local, inadequate transportation facilities, high cost of transportation, too much costly red-tape in starting any enterprise, lack of capital, and the natural antipathy of the Polish landed proprietors to trade and industry,

[35] Dr. Górski, pp. 35, 39, 40.
[36] Dr. L. Caro, p. 77.

commerce and industry have not been developed
properly in Poland.[37]

(e) Low wages and few working-days.—This state
of affairs was further aggravated by very low wages
paid for farm labor,[38] and by.numerous church holidays.[39] In the seventies of the last century, for instance, there were in 34 Galician counties 100-120
church holidays; in 22 counties, 120-150; and in 16
counties, 150-200; in the last case leaving only
about five months in the year for work. This surely
afforded the Galician peasant an inevitable and unsurpassed opportunity for fasting as well as for
praying.

Result—emigration.—In the light of this brief survey of the economic condition of the Polish peasantry, the Polish peasant's chief motive for emigration becomes clearly evident. The pressure of economic necessity was becoming too great for him to
bear it meekly any longer. Whether he wanted to,
or not, he had to go in search of better working and
living conditions.

Possibilities of improvement. (a) In agriculture.
—All this, however, does not mean that Poland is
unable to feed and keep in reasonable comfort her
population. Her territory has unlimited agricultural and mineral resources; all that is necessary is
to develop them properly. Given right political conditions and sufficient capital, her agriculture, her industry, and her commerce will rise and flourish, and
her children will have enough work at home and
bread to spare. In Galicia alone there are over
2,200,000 acres of land which could be brought under
cultivation by drainage, and would yield 5,000,000
quintals of grain, increasing the income from land
by 80,000,000 francs. Better feeding of cows and

[37] Dr. Górski, pp. 44-45; cf. also Van Norman, p. 33.
[38] Dr. Caro, p. 78.
[39] Ibidem, p. 78.

increasing the milk supply by one liter per cow daily, would give 55,000,000 francs annually. And by better feeding of the Galician pigs in order to get full price for them in the markets of Vienna or Prague, 10,000,000 francs more would be added to the Galician peasants' annual income. The Galician emigrants to Germany and America brought annually before the war thirty to forty million francs. This, even if continued, would not compare with what could be secured right at home by better and more intensive agriculture alone.[40]

(b) In industry.—Then, too, there are in Poland unlimited possibilities along the line of industrial expansion. The Poles realize this fully, and are making every effort to develop Polish industry. In the years 1902-10 in Galicia the number of factory workers increased 42%, machinery, measured by horse power, 65%, and the number of workers employed in 1910 in home-industries, as distinguished from factory industries, was 97,000 persons.[41] Factories, in the strict sense of the term, Galicia numbered in 1910-14, 363. The output of these in 1908-1914 increased from 300 to 500 million francs.[42] Moreover, in 1866 the Galician provincial budget included no appropriations for economic purposes, but in the provincial budget of 1911 these appropriations amounted to 14,191,237 crowns, or 22.39% of the general budget, and occupied the second place in the budget, yielding the first place to appropriations for educational purposes.[43]

All this shows that more and more industry is supplementing agriculture, and that Poland is undergoing a gradual transition from an agricultural to an industrial economy. The recent war retarded

[40] Dr. Górski, pp. 35-36.
[41] Kazimierz Bartoszewicz, Dzieje Galicji, p. 195.
[42] Dr. Górski, p. 57.
[43] Bartoszewicz, p. 179.

the process; but the new political status of Poland will in due time offset the retardation by accelerating the speed of the transformation. With this change the economic status of the Polish peasant will improve decidedly; and Polish emigration will diminish.

Polish peasant's education neglected.—During the nineteenth century the Polish peasant's education was sadly neglected. His masters, Russians, Prussians, and Austrians, the Polish landlords and the Polish clergy as well, were little concerned about his schooling. The less education he had, the more submissive he would be, the more easily ruled, and the more easily exploited. In Russian Poland it was a penal offense before the war to teach a Polish peasant anything in Polish; and not only that, but to teach him anything at all in any language, Polish or Russian. In Prussian Poland he might be taught, but there, again, he had to be taught only in German; and what he learned in a tongue unfamiliar to him, as well as obnoxious, because forced upon him, amounted to very little. In Austrian Poland attempts were made to give him systematic instruction, and to give it to him in his mother tongue. But for several decades the number of schools was inadequate to the population, many village communes remained without any schools, and thousands of peasant children were deprived of educational opportunities. Even as late as the close of the nineteenth century there were 4,117 schools, public and private, in Galicia, for 6,243 school communes, and out of 919,000 children between the ages of six to twelve years only 660,649 were attending any school.[44] Besides, many, if not most, of these schools

---

[44] Bartoszewicz, p. 183; cf. also Ency. Macierzy Szkolnej, II, p. 837.

were largely under the influence and control of the church, and consequently the training given the children in them was intended to fit them for the life hereafter rather than for life here and now. Mr. L. E. Van Norman gives a telling description of his visit to one such school for peasant children in Galicia. "Its sessions were held in a rustic little one-room building with the conventional thatched roof. The walls of this room, instead of being hung with geographical maps, charts, and other educational paraphernalia, were almost literally covered with portraits of Kaiser Franz Joseph, the late Kaiserin Elizabeth, and Prince Rudolph, and many different varieties of Catholic religious pictures. . . . The teacher was the village priest who made the children recite the catechism for my benefit, which they did in the most sing-song and unintelligible fashion. . . . They recited also verses from the saints, and then had some mental arithmetic. Finally, the prize scholar was asked where was America. He hesitated a moment, then said he did not know, except that it was far-off, and that it was the country to which good Polish boys went when they died. At the close a number of small religious pictures and prayer-books were distributed to the bright boys, and coral wreaths and rosaries to the girls." [45]

Result—illiteracy.—It is not to be wondered, therefore, that in 1900 the percentage of illiteracy in Galicia was 52% among the male and 59.99% among the female population, above six years of age.[46]

Growing improvement in education.—Yet we must not fail to see the progress that has been made along the line of peasant education in the last fifty years, and to note what a free people under normal

[45] Poland—the Knight among the Nations, pp. 243-244.
[46] Dr. Caro, p. 75.

conditions will do when it is free to act. In 1866
Galicia was granted provincial autonomy. At once
improvements along almost every line of public
betterment were begun, with education receiving first
attention. In 1868 for 6,243 school districts, village,
town, and city, there were only 2,476 elementary
schools of all kinds. By 1898 the number of elementary public schools increased to 4,117; by 1906 to
4,902; by 1913 to 5,963; and in 1914 the Council of
Public Education reported only 24 communes without an elementary school-commune having only 15-30
children of school age.[47]

The increase in the enrollment of children in
these elementary schools is also worthy of note. In
1871 the number of children in elementary schools
was 156,015; in 1898—660,649; in 1907—953,499;
and in 1913—1,152,048, with 216,778 children in supplementary schools, making a total of 1,368,826.[48]

Besides elementary day schools, Galicia has been
establishing supplementary industrial and voca-
tional schools. According to government reports
there were 134 such schools in the province in 1913
with a total attendance in 1911-12 of 12,569 pupils.[49]

Secondary and higher schools have been developed with equal energy. In 1868 Galicia had 12
gymnasia, with an eight-year course of study in
each, 7 with a four-year course in each, and 2 technical preparatory schools, one with a three-year
course of study, and the other with a six-year course.
The number of students in these institutions at
that time was 7,905. In 1910-11 the number of public gymnasia in Galicia was 86 and of technical preparatory schools—14, with a total attendance of
40,060 students. In addition to these there were 17
private gymnasia for men and 13 for women, with

[47] Bartoszewicz, p. 183.
[48] Ibidem, pp. 183-184.
[49] Dr. Górski, p. 46.

an enrollment of 4,110. The two universities of Cracow and Lwow had 1,822 students in 1880-81 and a faculty of 148 instructors, professors, and lecturers. In 1911-12 the enrollment of students in both universities was 8,088, and the faculties numbered 409 members.[50]

Education—first concern of new Poland.—Moreover, it is very gratifying to know that after the reconstitution of new Poland in 1918 one of the foremost concerns of the new Polish Government was the reëstablishment and reorganization of the school system of the country. The Poles fully realize that education of the rank and file of the people is one of the most important foundation stones of the New Republic. The effort is being also made to secularize the Polish schools, to give the Polish child an education free from ecclesiastical control and influence, which will adequately fit him for life.

Polish press.—A marked growth is manifest also in the Polish periodical press in Galicia. In 1865 the Polish press was represented by 14 publications, in 1875 by 68, in 1901 by 237, and in 1914 by 342. Among these there were 14 Polish dailies, published in Cracow and Lwow, with a total circulation of 140 thousand.[51]

Polish organizations.—Furthermore, the last fifty years have witnessed a remarkable increase in organizations of various kinds, political, educational, economic, philanthropic, et cetera. In 1874 Polish social interests and activities were represented by 590 organizations; in 1900 by 5,518; and in 1912 by 12,621. This last number included 3,956 educational organizations and libraries, 2,601 agricultural societies, and 1,077 industrial and commercial associations.[52]

[50] Bartoszewicz, pp. 182-183.
[51] Ibidem, p. 196.
[52] Ibidem, p. 196.

Living conditions: (a) Housing.—Living conditions of the Polish peasant are very simple. The houses are of stone, logs, or boards, plastered over with mud and white-washed. The roof is thatched or mud-covered, and over the mud is laid straw, upon which often grows moss, so that a peasant's hut, topped off with green-growing moss is a frequent picturesque addition to the landscape. The interior of the house is often divided into two rooms, in most cases separated by the main entrance and a hall running clear across to the other side of the house. One of the rooms constitutes the living, eating, and sleeping quarters for the family, in many instances for two and three families.[53] The other room, across the hall, furnishes shelter to the live-stock, and to the farm poultry. The peasant hut, though humble, is, in itself and alone, very picturesque. Surrounded by trees and separated from neighboring houses by little kitchen or flower gardens, it far surpasses for comfort and even health many a shack in some immigrant sections of our American cities. A Polish village with its picturesque houses and with their still more picturesque occupants, is, particularly on a Sunday or holiday, when the villagers turn out in their best, a sight long to be remembered.[54]

(b) Food.—The Polish peasant lives simply. The vegetables he raises in his garden furnish practically all his food. Potatoes are his great staple, but he is also fond of cabbage, beets, and beans, and he occasionally grows some corn. Of the cabbage he makes soups and pressed cakes. He has also a thick grain porridge, known as *kasza,* and he especially likes a soup made of red beets and known as *barszcz.* Meat is very scarce. He enjoys that delicacy only

[53] Postep, August, 1920, p. 176.
[54] Cf. Van Norman, pp. 234-235.

POLAND'S COUNTRY SIDE

    1. Ploughing with Oxen
    2. Farming with Machinery

[See page 38

PRINCIPAL SQUARE: CRACOW

A POLISH PEASANT HOME

[See page 48

in winter when he has killed a pig, or on holidays and on special festive occasions.[55]

(c) **Clothing.**—In summer the Polish peasant's clothing consists of thin shirt and trousers, home-made, and to this, in winter, he adds a sheepskin coat, with the fleece turned inside. He goes bare-footed most of the time, and frequently bareheaded. The *górale,* or mountain peasants, of the Carpathians have a particularly striking dress, and the simple yet impressive dignity of their carriage adds greatly to their picturesqueness.[56]

The lot of the Polish peasant woman.—The lot of the Polish peasant woman is somewhat hard and monotonous, but not necessarily unhappy. Her mental development may not be of a very high order, yet it is as good as her husband's for she has attended the same school together with him, and has enjoyed equal educational opportunities. She does a good deal of hard work, but in this respect she is cheerfully helping her husband in the common struggle for existence. Her life is dull and dreary, but not any more so than her husband's. The Polish peasant woman, therefore, simply shares the common lot of the social class to which she belongs.

Recreation.—Too much work and no play makes Jack a dull boy regardless of his nationality or his social position. So the Polish peasant, too, looks for recreation and amusement, and finds it in frequent informal neighborly visits, village dances, weddings, christenings, church fairs, and in holiday festivities of one kind or another. He loves music passionately, and delights in dancing thoroughly.

Group life, national consciousness, patriotism.—Group life among the Polish peasants is very strong, national consciousness intense, and patriotism very

[55] Cf. Van Norman, p. 236, and N. O. Winter, p. 266.
[56] The same authors, pp. 236 and 266, respectively.

ardent. Commonly the Poles are regarded as individualists of an extreme type. The fact is overlooked that they act in groups. The Polish peasant does whatever the group does; and nothing can move him as long as the group refuses to act. To bear this fact in mind is of utmost importance in dealings with the Poles, especially in social and religious work among the Polish immigrants in this country. No enterprise of any kind may reasonably look for success among them unless it takes their group-life into *account,* and tries to make a successful appeal to the group.

Owing to the determined efforts of Poland's partitioners to denationalize the Poles and to stamp out their language, the Polish peasant's national consciousness and patriotism have been developed to a high degree; and therefore he clings to his traditions and to his language tenaciously. In the period of dismemberment the Poles found their native tongue the strongest bond of union. The Polish peasant, says Van Norman, is patriotism personified. He has responded nobly to every call of his country in her hour of need. In the Kosciuszko insurrection he cheerfully left his field, and, armed only with his scythe, he went forth to battle. He has been as responsive ever since. He is the most common-sense, practical peasant in the world. He is also self-respecting, independent, strong, and usually moral, temperate, and cheerful. He is the hope of his nation. The regeneration and progress of the nation, political, social, or religious, must come from the peasant.[57] So it is. The Polish peasant is determining today Poland's future. He holds the balance of power in the Polish Diet today; and one of the recent Premiers of Poland, Witos, was a peasant.

[57] Poland—The Knight among the Nations, p. 233.

The development of Christianity in Poland.—
Christianity in its western form was introduced into
Poland in 966 by Poland's first historical ruler,
Mieszko I (960-992). His motive for the acceptance of Christianity and for its introduction into
his dominions was a desire to save his country from
devastating German wars, carried, 'on under the
guise of Christianizing the pagan Slavs. The first
bishopric was established by the same ruler in 968
in Poznzń. The Archbishopric of Gniezno was
founded about the year 1000 by Boleslaw I the
Brave, 992-1025, with the consent of the German
Emperor Otto III. This step made Poland independent of Germany ecclesiastically. At the same
time a number of new bishoprics were established
in newly conquered territories; at Colberg in Pomerania, at Cracow in Little Poland, and at Breslau
in Silesia. Monastic Orders were invited to settle in
Poland, and were given large grants of land together with special privileges. With the assistance
of the political power Christianity spread throughout Poland very rapidly, and the influence of the
Church and its clergy soon made itself felt in the
State. By 1180 the higher clergy were invited to
participate in the King's Council; and by 1206, owing to the adoption of the Gregorian reforms in Poland, the nomination of bishops, heretofore a prerogative of the Polish kings, passed over to the
Pope. The Church was now supreme in Poland,—
a supremacy which it enjoyed and made full use of
for over two centuries and a half, until the reign of
Kazimir IV Jagiellończyk (1447-1492), when the
right of episcopal nominations was regained by
Kazimir, and henceforth remained a prerogative of
the Polish Crown.

Hussitism in Poland.—The Hussite movement, which in the fifteenth century kept Bohemia in commotion, found its way also to Poland. The Polish clergy was at the height of its power and its pretensions. As a consequence the Polish nobility was irritated, indignant, and jealous. Moreover, the Poles had had enough of Germany. Hussitism, therefore, both as a religion and as a nationalistic movement appealed to the Poles and was welcomed by them. Many wealthy and influential families, especially in Great Poland, became its adherents and sympathizers. With the defeat of the Hussites in Bohemia, the movement was suppressed in Poland for a time. But in the sixteenth century, under the influence of the Reformation, it revived again, and its adherents were known then as the Bohemian Brethren.

The Reformation found in Poland a fertile, but rather rocky soil without depth. Its ideas struck root quickly, but not deeply. They found ready acceptance with the city population and with the nobility, the upper crust of society, but failed to penetrate into the lower social strata, the depths of the peasantry. The movement, therefore, was doomed to a short life from the start. For a time, however, the Reformation was very popular with the upper classes; in fact so popular that all kinds and shades of religious reformers found refuge and welcome in the country. Most influential were Lutheranism, Calvinism, and Antitrinitarianism. Drawing its inspiration from the Reformation, there sprang up also a short-lived movement tending in the direction of a National Church. But as in the fifteenth century in the case of Hussitism, so now again in the case of the Reformation the Catholic reactionaries, under the leadership of the Jesuits, and supported by reactionary kings, succeeded in getting the upper hand, checked the movement, and in the course of the seventeenth and eighteenth centuries well-nigh exterminated it.

Relative strength of religious faiths in Poland.— The relative strength of existing faiths in Poland in 1791, just before the second partition, was as follows:—

Roman Catholics 53.2%
Uniates 29.2%
Disuniates 3.2%
Hebrews 10.5%
Protestants 1.7%
Dissidents from the Russian Orthodox Church...... 1.1%
Arminians 0.5%
Mohammedans .... 0.6% [58]

These relative proportions have been considerably modified in the course of a century and a quarter. The Protestants have evidently grown in strength; for they are now estimated to form 6.6% of the total population.[59] Nevertheless the old statistics are still fairly indicative of the relative strength of the different religious faiths in Poland today. The Catholics, Roman, Greek, Uniate, about 79.4% strong, are greatly in the lead; next come the Jews, about 12% strong; then—the Protestants, numbering 6.6%; finally—the Russian Dissidents, Armenians, and Mohammedans making up 2%.

The attitude of the Polish people toward institutional religion.—The attitude of the Polish people toward institutional religion is of interest. The chief emphasis placed by both Catholics and Protestants on dogma and ritual rather than on life has resulted in estrangement of the educated classes from the Church and in blind superstitious devotion of the masses. It is fair to say that the educated Poles, whether Catholic or Protestant, are

[58] Tadeusz Korzon, Wewnętrzne Dzieje Polski, I, Table attached to p. 320.
[59] Jakob Glass, Ewangelicy Polacy, pp. 8-12. The Centenary Bulletin, M. E., Nashville, October, 1920, p. 2.

largely indifferent to the Church. They regard themselves as having outgrown religion, and consequently do not care to bother about it any more. Especially is this true of those brought up in Catholicism; less true of those brought up in Protestantism.

With the masses the case is quite different. The vital, characteristic fact of the Polish peasant's life is his religion. He is perhaps the most devout peasant in the world, and, beyond a doubt, is the most faithful as well as one of the most superstitious of all the adherents of the Church of Rome. Most of the legends and general folk-lore of the peasant are religious in character, having their origin in his love and reverence for the Blessed Virgin. "Matka Boska," the Mother of God, as the peasants affectionately call her, is the ideal of all that is beautiful, the refuge, the protector, the constant intercessor of the sinful and the oppressed, and the Queen of the Polish nation. The Polish priest is identified with every phase of the peasant life, and there are no festivities in which he does not take a part. He is looked up to as the guide and guardian of his flock, and is regarded and treated with utmost deference by his parishioners. It cannot be said that in his personal life he always sets an ideal example.[60]

The average Protestant Pole lacks none of his Catholic brother's religious fervor and devotion, while his religion is of a higher order, less superstitious, more intelligent, and more spiritual.

Poland's religious needs.—The most imperative religious needs of the Poland of today are: separation of Church and State, liberation of the soul of the Polish people from the domination of medieval religious conceptions and superstitions, revitalization and spiritualization of Poland's religious life.

[60] See Van Norman, p. 245, and Winter, p. 276.

CHAPTER II: POLISH IMMIGRATION TO THE UNITED STATES AND ITS DISTRIBUTION

Chapter II

POLISH IMMIGRATION TO THE UNITED STATES AND ITS DISTRIBUTION

History of Polish immigration. (a) Early immigration.—Polish immigration to the United States dates as far back as the first half of the seventeenth century, when the Zborowski, or Zabrisky, family came to this country, and settled near Hackensack, N. J. Martin Zborowski, a lawyer by profession, made a big fortune in real estate, which in 1878 he left to his son, William Elliot Zborowski. William Elliot married Carey's daughter, whose mother was an Astor, and, dying accidentally in 1903, he left a fortune of $10,000,000. William Elliot's sister, Anna, married Baron Fontenoy. The Zborowskis are the oldest Polish family in the United States.[1]

Other Poles soon followed. According to Father J. Conway, "as early as 1659 the Dutch colonists of Manhattan Island hired a Polish schoolmaster for the education of the youth of the community."[2] During the Revolutionary War came the well-known patriots, Kosciuszko and Pulaski; after the war came the writer and poet, Niemcewicz; and later— Prince Dimitrius A. Galiczyn, who, assuming the name of John Smith, entered the priesthood, was consecrated by Bishop Carroll, of Baltimore, March 16th, 1795, and settled in the parish of "Bohemia Manor," Cecil Co., Maryland.[3] The unsuccessful insurrection of 1830-31 led many Poles by way of

[1] Rev. Waclaw Kruszka, Hist. Polska w Ameryce, I, pp. 53-54.
[2] Ibidem, I, p. 53.
[3] Ibidem, I, pp. 63-64.

France and England to seek refuge in this country. The same thing happened in 1848 and in 1863. In 1854 under the leadership of Father Leopold Moczygemba a number of peasant families from Upper Silesia came and settled in Texas, at a place which they named "Panna Marya"—that is, Virgin Mary.[4]

(b) **Later immigration.**—Polish immigration to the United States on a large scale, however, does not begin until in the seventies of the nineteenth century, following the Franco-Prussian War. Its original source was Prussian Poland—Upper Silesia, Poznania, and West Prussia. Beginning somewhat slowly at first in the seventies the stream of Polish immigration swelled and spread to such proportions as to sweep away with it not only the natural increase of the peasant population, but also a portion of the normal population of these provinces. So that in the next decade, 1882-1895, in Poznania and in West Prussia, the normal population was actually reduced by 41,000.[5] From Prussian Poland the emigration movement spread gradually to Russian Poland, and thence to Galicia. Polish emigration from Galicia does not assume any considerable proportions until the nineties of the last century.

Volume of Polish immigration.—The volume of Polish immigration was greatest in the decade and a half preceding the World War. In 1901-1910 the number of Polish immigrants to the United States was 873,669. For the period 1904-1913 it was 1,009,054. The year 1912-13 was the banner year, bringing 174,365 Polish immigrants. The year 1914 yielded 122,657, and the year 1915 only 9,065.[6]

---

[4] Kruszka, I, pp. 71, 75; Emily Balch, Our Slavic Fellow Citizens, p. 228.

[5] Okolowicz, Wychodżtwo polskie, p. 23.

[6] Ibidem, pp. 21-25; Dr. Caro, p. 34; Report of Com. Gen. of Immig., 1912-13.

General causes of Polish immigration.—The general causes of Polish immigration to the United States, according to Mr. Joseph Okolowicz and Prof. L. Caro, both of whom are first-class authorities on this particular subject, are (1) overpopulation of the Polish village by an agricultural proletariat or semi-proletariat; (2) small landholdings, primitive agricultural methods, and meager productivity of the soil; (3) insufficient industrial development; (4) low wages; (5) excessive taxation; (6) alcoholism and petty litigations; (7) land-hunger and the difficulty to satisfy it at home; and (8) emigration propaganda carried on by agents of steamship companies, by representatives of foreign governments and corporations, and by lucky emigrants themselves.

Special causes.—Besides these general causes of Polish emigration to the United States, there were special, immediate causes operating in each section of the country. For instance, the immediate causes of Polish emigration from Prussian Poland in the seventies and eighties were greater economic backwardness of the country at that time, intelligence due to better common school education, linguistic and religious persecution resulting from Bismarck's "Kultur-kampf" policy, and the contagious influence of German emigration. Polish emigration from Russian Poland began in 1876. The immediate causes back of it were a crop failure, a crisis and lockout in the textile industry, throwing hundreds of men out of work, and the introduction of universal military service, in that year.[7] Polish emigration from Galicia seems to have been due largely to the operation of the more general causes and economic conditions enumerated in the above section.

[7] Okolowicz, pp. 22-23; see also Hourwich, Immigration, pp. 14, 190.

Character of Polish immigration.—The character of Polish immigration may be determined by the following statistical facts. The Polish emigrants leaving Russian Poland in 1912 with the intention of establishing permanent homes abroad were divided as to (1) *social classes:* landless peasants 50.7%, landed peasants 27.1%, factory workmen 3.3%, other occupations 18.9%; (2) *literacy:* unable to read or write: men 17.95%, women 11.66%, total 29.61%; (3) *occupations:* farm laborers 47.15%, unskilled laborers 28.41%, without occupation to include women and children 18.55%, skilled workmen 5.35%, professional, literary, and business 0.54%; (4) *sex:* men 66.3%, women 33.7%; (5) *family relationship:* single individuals 47%, married 35.6%, children 17.4%; (6) *religion:* Catholics 76.1%, Jews 15.3%, Orthodox 3%, and Protestants 5.6%.[8] According to the findings of the American Immigration Commission the percentage of illiteracy among the Poles of both sexes is only 24.5%; in respect of occupations in this country they are divided as follows: farmers 5.7%, business, professional, and clerical 8.7%, skilled trades 5.1%, mine, mill, and factory workers 23.2%, laborers, not on farms 29.1%, all others 28.2%; and 77% of the married Poles have their wives in this country, over against 23% whose wives are abroad.[9] This last fact is an evidence that the Poles constitute a permanent factor of our population, and possess qualities of value to any community. They are not transient squatters, but come with the expectation, hope, and purpose of making permanent homes."[10] The permanent character of Polish immigrants to the U. S. is further shown by statistics of visits made abroad

---

[8] Okolowicz, pp. 28, 32, 33-34; Report of Com. Gen. of Immig., 1912-13.
[9] Jenks and Lauck, Immigration, pp. 417, 433; Hourwich, p. 171.
[10] Balch, pp. 473-74; Winter, p. 325.

by foreign-born employes in iron and steel mills. Of the Slovaks 21.4% make such visits home; of the Hungarians—20.3%; of the Russians—10.2%; of the Bohemians and Moravians—8.5%; and of the Poles only 6.6%.[11] As workers the Polish immigrants are both capable and industrious. Of Polish adult male clothing workers, 18 years of age and over, residing in the United States less than five years, 37.4% are reported by the Immigration Commission as having made less than $10 per week, 54.1% between $10 to $15 per week, and 8.5%—$15 and over, whereas of German clothing workers 40% averaged less than $10 per week, 51.4%—$10 to $15 per week, and 8.6%—$15 and over, or, even in this last instance, only one-tenth of one per cent of German clothing workers as compared with Polish clothing workers averaged the highest wage. The same is true of Polish women and girls in the same industry. The majority of them (55.4%) earned more than $7.50 per week, while the majority of American women of native parentage (57.2%) earned less than that amount. Polish girls, between the ages of 14 and 18, earned on an average $5.25 per week, whereas native American girls of native parentage made only $5.02 per week.[12] These wages were, of course, pre-war wages. The Polish immigrant, therefore, taking him all around, is not half as bad as he is sometimes imagined and represented to be.

Distribution and location of Polish immigrants.— According to the Polish National Alliance Calendar for 1910, there were approximately 3,063,000 Poles in the United States at that time, and their distribution was as follows:

[11] Hourwich, p. 75.
[12] Ibidem, pp. 370-371; Immig. Com. Reports, II, pp. 293, 301.

	Total Population	No. of Poles	ercentage
Pennsylvania	6,302,115	500,000	8.
New York	7,268,894	475,000	6.5
Illinois	4,821,550	475,000	9.5
Wisconsin	2,069,042	250,000	12.
Michigan	2,420,982	240,000	10.
Massachusetts	2,805,346	240,000	8.75
Ohio	4,157,515	200,000	5.
New Jersey	1,883,669	120,000	6.
Minnesota	1,751,394	120,000	6.
Connecticut	908,420	120,000	13.
Indiana	2,516,462	50,000	2.5
Missouri	3,106,665	40,000	1.5
Maryland	1,188,044	30,000	2.5
Nebraska	1,066,300	25,000	2.
Texas	3,048,710	25,000	0.8
Rhode Island	428,556	25,000	5.
Delaware	184,735	20,000	11.
Maine	694,466	20,000	3.
West Virginia	958,800	15,000	1.5
Washington	518,103	12,000	2.
California	1,485,053	15,000	1.
New Hampshire	411,588	12,000	2.5
North Dakota	319,146	12,000	6.
Kansas	1,470,495	12,000	0.8
Other States	———	10,000	—
Total		3,063,000	

These figures, however, are very conservative and unquestionably below the actual numbers of Poles in the given States, particularly some of them. The American Association of Foreign-Language Newspapers in its statistical report of 1919 estimates the number of Poles in the United States at 3,595,000; and the Polish Press, as early as 1908, estimated that there were about 4,000,000 Poles in the United States at that time. The estimate of the American Association of Foreign Language Newspapers is probably nearest the actual fact.[13]

The above table makes it clear that the North Atlantic States and the States around the Great

[13] Statistical Report, August, 1919, cited by Okolowicz, p. 36; Dr. Caro, p. 115; Note 1, and Statistical Table, pp. 117-118; Archibald McClure, Leadership of the New America, p. 69.

Lakes constitute the region in which the Poles have largely settled. This has been due to the industrial development of these states, favorable agricultural conditions, especially in such states as Wisconsin and Minnesota, and to the prevailing climate throughout this region.

Of the large cities the following are the great Polish centers: Chicago 400,000; Detroit 100,000; Milwaukee 100,000; Buffalo 100,000; Toledo 30,000; Cleveland 50,000; Pittsburgh and vicinity 200,000; New York 200,000; Philadelphia 50,000; Baltimore 35,000; and Boston 25,000.

Migration of Poles in the United States.—The Polish immigrants constitute a reasonably stable element in the population of a community. "They are not transient squatters," says the Boston *Transcript,* "but come with the expectation, hope, and purpose of making permanent homes." [14] To be sure, there is some migration incidental to changing industrial conditions and to the natural human desire of seeing the country. In such cases, however, the first ones to move on are the single individuals and the married men whose families are abroad. The men with families usually stay, unless absolutely forced by prolonged local unemployment to make a change. The Polish immigrant has no Bohemian habits; he does not fancy moving from place to place all the time. He likes to settle down and stay. This statement finds support also in the discovery made by the Roosevelt Immigration Commission that over three-fourths of newly arrived immigrants, including the Poles, have spent the entire period of their residence since their arrival in the United States in the neighborhood of where they now live.[15] Polish settlements, therefore, do not fluctuate; they are

[14] August 4, 1909.
[15] Jenks and Lauck, Immigration, p. 127.

reasonably stable and growing. And the majority of the Poles own their homes.

Return movement.—During the last two years, since the restoration of Poland as an independent state, there has been, to be sure, a good deal of restlessness among the Polish immigrants in this country, and quite a strong tendency toward re-emigration to Poland. Thousands have been planning to return, and thousands have actually returned. From June, 1918, to June, 1920, 365,367 aliens left America for Europe, among whom were 18,545 Poles. (From January to March, 1920, the number of aliens emigrating from America was 61,000, the majority of whom were Czechoslovaks and Poles.) [16] It is not likely, however, that this return movement among the Poles will assume large proportions. Many will be held back by ties, either economic or social. Of the re-emigrants many have gone because of family or business reasons; others from motives of sentiment and patriotism. But many of those that have gone over have already signified their desire to return to America.[17] Indications are that the Polish re-emigration movement has already spent its force. It is fair to conclude that economic and social causes will, as usual, operate powerfully to hold the majority of the Poles here to their respective places.

Prospect for new immigration.—As to fresh immigration from Poland, it is doubtful that this will be very large in the future. For the next few years, before Poland is able to reorganize and rebuild its economic life, many will, probably, seek refuge and opportunity in this country. But as Poland's economic life becomes reconstructed, Polish immigration will gradually diminish. According to some reports Polish emigrants to America are pouring into

[16] "Foreign-Born," for May, 1920, p. 22.
[17] "Codz. Kurjer Narodowy," for October, 1920.

Danzig at the rate of 250 families, or 1,000 souls, daily. That the movement is gaining volume, there seems to be no doubt. To house the steady stream of emigrants while waiting for steamers, the Danzig authorities have long since established an embarkation camp in the outskirts of the city with accommodations for 4,000. The new flood of refugees fleeing before the Bolshevist invasion filled this to overflowing in a trice. A second camp, housing 2,000, was opened and as quickly filled. A third camp is being opened in the old quarantine barracks. And seeing no prospect of the cessation of emigration, the authorities are casting about for still further accommodations.[18] However, 95% of the present emigration from Poland is Jewish rather than Polish.[19] This small percentage of native Poles among the present emigrants from Poland to America is rather significant and doubtless indicative of the future.

[18] "Foreign-Born," September-October, 1920, p. 14.
[19] "Codz. Kurjer Ludowy," for October, 1920.

CHAPTER III: ECONOMIC CONDITIONS OF POLISH IMMIGRANTS IN THE UNITED STATES

Chapter III

ECONOMIC CONDITIONS OF POLISH IMMIGRANTS IN THE UNITED STATES

Means of livelihood.—As has been previously indicated, the majority of Polish immigrants to this country belong to the class of unskilled labor. According to the findings of the Immigration Commission, 6.4% are in the trades, 3.8% in domestic and personal service, and the rest in unskilled labor.[1] However, the Poles are not afraid of work; they know how to apply themselves, and they do it with determination and endurance. They are found in nearly every industry of importance, in mining, steel and glass industries, textile mills, boots and shoes and clothing manufacturing, stock-yards and packing houses, agricultural implement and vehicle establishments, automobile shops, furniture factories, wire works, oil and sugar refineries, and in agriculture.[2]

Wages.—The wages of the Polish immigrants have, more or less, been the prevailing wages in given industries at a given time. In this connection it is of great interest to see the weekly and yearly earnings of native and foreign-born workers in a number of leading industries, before the War, and to note the relative differences. As in these industries Poles are found in considerable numbers, the schedules represent their pre-war wages in those industries.

[1] Jenks and Lauck, p. 124.
[2] Ibidem, p. 139; Balch, pp. 282-3.

AVERAGE AMOUNT OF WEEKLY EARNINGS OF MALE EMPLOYEES, 18 YEARS AND OVER [3]

Industry	Native-Born		Foreign-Born
	Native Father	Foreign Father	
Agricultural Implements and Vehicles	$13.23	$13.62	$12.89
Boots and Shoes	12.57	12.84	11.19
Clothing	14.59	15.66	12.91
Cotton Goods	11.60	10.45	9.28
Furniture	11.43	12.31	11.58
Glass Industry—Bottles	16.87	19.54	12.63
Iron and Steel	16.54	16.62	13.29
Leather	11.02	12.15	10.27
Oil Refining	14.83	13.67	13.71
Sugar Refining	13.42	13.12	11.64
Woolen and Worsted Goods	11.62	11.74	9.96

AVERAGE AMOUNT OF WEEKLY EARNINGS OF FEMALE EMPLOYEES, 18 YEARS AND OVER [3]

Industry	Native-Born		Foreign-Born
	Native Father	Foreign Father	
Agricultural Implements and Vehicles	$7.13	$7.26	$7.12
Boots and Shoes	7.98	8.60	7.89
Clothing	7.41	8.60	7.74
Collars, Cuffs and Shirts	7.47	7.78	7.77
Cotton Goods	8.34	7.96	7.93
Glass Tableware	5.61	5.71	5.14
Leather	7.13	7.39	6.39
Woolen and Worsted Goods	8.35	8.61	7.96
Gloves	6.37	6.88	6.55

The average pre-war yearly earnings of the native-born, investigated by the Immigration Commission, were $533; of the foreign-born—$385; while of the native-born of foreign fathers they were $526. This shows that, while the difference in the annual earnings of the native-born and the foreign-born is considerable, the earnings of the native-born of foreign fathers are nearly on a par with the earnings of the native-born of native fathers. In other words, the second generation of the immigrants rises to the productive level of native Americans. Of the more recent immigrants the average annual earnings were

[3] Jenks and Lauck, pp. 147, 149.

as follows: Of the North Italians $425, of the South Italians $368, of the Poles $365, of the Servians $325, and of the Syrians $321. And the average annual earnings of Polish women were $200.[4] The Poles, then, occupy a middle position among the newer groups of immigrants with reference to earning capacity.

Other sources of income.—That the pre-war average annual earnings of the representatives of Polish families were inadequate for family support requires no proof. That the earnings of the father had to be suplemented by additional earnings of the mother, or of the children, or of both, is plainly evident. Thus we find in the Report of the Immigration Commission that of the Polish households studied 35.8% of families had their entire income from husband; 8.5% from husband and children; 13.2% from unspecified sources; and 37.7% from husband and boarders and lodgers.[5]

Polish women in industry.—Owing to this condition, large numbers of Polish women and girls are found in various industries such as textile mills, clothing factories, cigar factories, packing houses, and canneries. The Polish women enjoy the same reputation that the Polish men have for willingness to work hard. A determination to work and earn and save is uppermost with them. Marriage is not suffered to be a bar to work. They have, therefore, made their way into a wide circle of industries; and in some of these, as we have seen, they have been making fairly good wages.[6]

Standard of living of Polish industrial workers.—The Poles, together with other recent immigrants, are frequently blamed for their low standard of living. It is forgotten that their low standard of living

[4] Jenks and Lauck, pp. 126, 127.
[5] Ibidem, p. 160.
[6] Cf. Balch, pp. 354, 355-357.

is imposed upon them rather than of their own choosing, and that it is not a permanent, but only a temporary characteristic. A new immigrant in a strange country, unacquainted with the language, customs, and conditions of the land, with no resources but his immediate earnings to depend upon for his daily bread in season of employment and out of season, does not have many choices left as to the kind of work he will do, the amount of pay he must have for it, and the kind of house and community he will live in. By sheer and inevitable necessity he is forced to take whatever work he can get, to be satisfied with whatever wages his generous employer is willing to pay him, and to be contented with such food and shelter as his wages allow, leaving a small margin of savings against emergencies. In the course of time, as his economic condition improves, his standard of living naturally rises. Temporarily, however, "sausage, and three loaves of stale bread for five cents" must be his staple food as long as his American Christian employer has the conscience to pay him the lowest possible wage for his labor, saying, "they're glad enough to get work." [7] To blame the Polish immigrant for his low standard of living under such conditions betrays a sad lack of judgment. We might with equal reason blame the early Virginia colonists for the unsanitary conditions which caused them to die of fever; the Pilgrims for their lack of foresight, energy, and efficiency, which brought about practical starvation of many of them; Lincoln for having been born in a log-cabin; Garfield for having been a mule driver; and President Harding for having started as a newsboy and a printer. Then, too, says Dr. Hourwich, "it is clearly insufficient to compare the sections inhabited by English-speaking skilled mechanics and their families with the settlements of the unskilled

[7] Shriver, pp. 27-28.

Slav laborers, with a view to showing that the former present a better appearance than the latter. The housing conditions of the new immigrants should be compared with those of the Irish and German unskilled laborers a generation ago, in order to support the conclusion that the former have introduced a lower standard of living."[8]

Poles in agriculture.—The Poles, however, are not all in cities and in factories. They are chiefly peasants, and many of them seek the country and take to farming. Miss Balch estimates that one-third of the Poles are living in country places; Rev. Father Kruszka puts the number at 500,000.[9] Miss Balch doubtless overestimates and Father Kruszka underestimates the number of Poles engaged in agriculture. The number probably is somewhere in the neighborhood of 750,000.

Polish farming communities are located in Massachusetts, New York, Ohio, Indiana, Illinois, Wisconsin, and Texas.[10] In 1901 the number of Polish farming settlements was estimated at seven hundred. The size of Polish farms varied from 40 to 360 acres and more, with an average of 80 acres. The total acreage of Polish farm land at that time was about 5,600,000. The value of these farms was put at $210,000,000.[11] By today these Polish agricultural settlements have considerably increased, if not in number, certainly in size, in population, and in the value of farms and farming equipment. If twenty years ago the value of Polish farms was $210,000,000, which certainly was a very modest estimate even at that time, averaging only $37.50 per acre, it is perfectly safe to say that today the value of Polish farm property, including land, build-

---

[8] Immigration, p. 54.
[9] Balch, p. 320; Kruszka, III, p. 120.
[10] Shriver, pp. 82-83; Jenks, p. 89.
[11] Kruszka, III, pp. 120-121.

ings, stock, and equipment, is at least twice that amount, or $420,000,000.

Transition to agriculture.—The Poles in the rural communities on Long Island and in the Connecticut Valley are of three classes, farm laborers, renters, and independent farmers. Their economic progress follows two lines; those who settle on the land immediately after their arrival in America, begin as farm laborers, gradually develop into renters, and finally become independent farm owners; a second class settle on the land after a number of years' residence and work in the city, and according to their accumulated savings begin either as renters, or at once as independent farm owners. However, the transition from industry to farming is slight; and wherever it is made, it must be made by the first generation of immigrants. The second generation, brought up in the city, are not likely to turn to farming as they grow up. Their associations, ambitions, and habits will be of the town.[12] According to the Immigration Commission, about one-half of the Polish farmers have been in this country less than a decade, at the time of the investigation made.[13] This shows that those who settled on farms did so either immediately on arrival or shortly after.

Poles efficient and successful farmers.—"The farming of the Poles," says Miss Balch, "is regarded as inferior by the Americans." Their great economic advantage is ascribed to the fact "that all the members of the family, women and children as well as men, work in the fields."[14] The fact, however, remains that the Poles are making a success of farms given up by the natives. "Their readiness in mastering the art of farming speaks well for their quickness of observation and their power to

[12] See Balch, p. 335.
[13] Jenks, p. 81.
[14] Our Slavic Fellow Citizens, p. 329.

apply information, and to adjust themselves to new conditions."[15] They understand intensive agriculture, and are industrious. They possess in extraordinary measure the qualities of application and endurance. They are thrifty and let little go to waste. Their success, accordingly, is no matter of surprise. The New Englanders of the Connecticut Valley, for instance, speak unhesitatingly in terms of highest praise of the industry, thrift, efficiency, and prosperity of the Polish farmers; and one after another of the best farms in the Connecticut Valley is passing into Polish hands.[16]

Poles in business.—During the early stages of Polish immigration, the Poles constituted chiefly an army of workers, seeking employment wherever it could be found. This was perfectly natural. Most of the Polish immigrants were peasants, without any qualifications for business and without any working capital. The first thing they had to do was to get a firm footing in their new land, to establish a home, and to accumulate some surplus capital. This having been done, they gradually began to branch out into business and manufacturing. Beginning cautiously, they started to use their working capital first in small enterprises and later on in larger undertakings. As time went on ever larger numbers would leave their factory jobs, and go into business for themselves. In this way Polish business grew and developed until today it is in a very flourishing condition, with full promise of still greater development. In every Polish colony one can today find numerous Polish stores, covering practically all branches of business; and some of these Polish business enterprises rival in variety, quantity, and quality of stock and in prices some of the better up-town American stores. As a result of high wages during

[15] Boston *Transcript*, August 4, 1909.
[16] See Shriver, pp. 82-85.

the War, and consequent greater accumulations of surplus capital, as well as the allurement of great business profits, the last five years have witnessed a tremendous development of Polish business. If it is safe to generalize from the observation of some settlements, it may be perfectly safe to say that Polish business has grown one hundred per cent and more in the last five years.

Poles in industry.—Besides business, the Poles have by degrees engaged in manufacturing. Here, too, Polish industry has been subject to a process of development. Starting on a small scale, and along few lines at first, it has slowly grown larger until it has come to embrace many lines of manufacturing today. The oldest Polish industry in the United States is the clothing industry. It dates back to the Civil War. The cause of its rise is evidently to be looked for in the large demand for clothing at that time, as during the recent World War, and in the resulting high wages and big profits.[17] Next, in point of time, engaging the attention of the Poles, is contracting and building and the moving of houses; then the brewing of beer, the manufacture of cigars and smoking tobacco, baking and butchering; and in more recent years the manufacture of picture frames, stained-glass windows, stoves, furniture, shoes, shirts, ties, and caps. As Polish business, so Polish industry has been greatly stimulated and has taken big strides forward in the last five years.

The Poles in the professions.—During the first twenty to thirty years of the early history of Polish immigration to the United States there was a great scarcity of professional men in every Polish settlement. The Polish immigrant, in need of professional services, had to resort to physicians and lawyers of other nationalities, particularly Jews. This

[17] Kruszka, III, pp. 92, 99.

state of things was inevitable. Polish immigration, as has already been noted, was not composed of the "inteligencja," including the professional class, but of the peasantry. It was only here and there that a professional man ventured to pull up stakes and transplant himself to the United States; and in such cases he very likely was the least desirable. Consequently the Polish immigrants in the United States had to wait until they could develop a professional class of their own from among the younger generation. This, again, required time. It is not to be wondered at, therefore, if for the first twenty-five to thirty years, that is, down to 1900 or 1905, the Polish colonies did not compare favorably, in respect of business, manufacturing, or the professions, with colonies of other earlier settlers, the Germans or even the Czechs. Such comparisons, though frequently made to the inevitable discredit of the Poles, have been very unfair; for they have never taken all the facts involved in the case into account. Given necessary time, however, the Polish peasant immigrants have gradually developed from among their own group a creditable business and professional class,—a class of business and professional men brought up in our American atmosphere and trained in our American institutions, wide-awake, energetic, and increasingly efficient, with qualities for service and leadership.

Value of Polish property.—Besides being industrious, the Polish immigrants are a very thrifty class of people. In the homeland the Polish peasant's one supreme ambition is to own a piece of land and a home. When he comes to America, he brings that supreme ambition with him. He works, denies himself, and saves, in order that he may some day have a home of his own to live in, and a patch of ground for that home to stand on.[18] Being more or

[18] Cf. Balch, p. 307.

less permanent residents, the Poles are owners of homes. It may safely be said that seventy to eighty per cent of them own their homes. As early as 1887 the Chicago *Tribune* calculated that the Poles in that one city owned real estate worth $10,000,000. In 1900 Father Kruszka estimated that the Poles in the United States owned $600,000,000 worth of city property alone, besides $210,000,000 worth of farm property. Today, taking into account the increase in population, the high wages and profits received during the War, and the fabulous increase in property values, it is safe to increase the former figure by 150%, raising the present value of Polish-owned city property to $1,500,000,000. To this let us add the minimum present value of Polish-owned farm property, namely, $420,000,000, and we have a moderate grand total of $1,920,000,000 worth of real estate property owned by the Poles in the United States.

Nor is this all. "Aside from their private banks, and state banks under their own management, the Poles have innumerable Building and Loan Associations, which play a large part in the savings and real estate developments. These associations are to be found in every Polish community, lending money, selling shares, carrying mortgages; in the cities covered by this report there are about 150 such organizations doing an annual business of about $7,000,000. One association in Buffalo showed a total of $91,000 handled in small sums for investors in the year 1913; and the same board of directors stated that there was no reason why that association should not carry in that community a business investment amounting to $960,000, all in small sums invested in stores, homes, and real estate. In Cleveland there is a Polish Chamber of Commerce, formed for the express purpose of 'booming Polish trade, influencing permanent settlement in the community, promoting sympathetic relations between the Poles and the Americans of other nationalities in that city.' "[19] In Chicago, in 1904, there were eighty-one Bohemian and Polish Building, Loan, and Homestead Associations with $6,200,000 in assets, 220,000 shares in force, and an approximate membership of 28,000.[20] In Baltimore, in 1920, the assets of five Polish Building and Loan Associations amounted to more than $2,000,000. And during the War the Poles purchased $67,000,000 worth of Liberty Bonds, receiving the fourth place among the subscribers of foreign birth or descent to the Liberty Loans.

[19] Hayden, Religious Work among Poles in America, pp. 9-10.
[20] Balch, p. 307.

CHAPTER IV: SOCIAL CONDITIONS AND EDU-
CATIONAL FORCES

Chapter IV

SOCIAL CONDITIONS AND EDUCATIONAL FORCES

Housing.—In a study of social conditions of different social or racial groups, it is well to begin with the home, the housing conditions; for the home, its structure, location, environment, and arrangement, is, broadly and relatively speaking, both an embodiment and an expression of the social ideals and tastes of any given social group as well as a primary social institution the general character and atmosphere of which powerfully influence and mold the lives of coming generations. Housing conditions, however, are not, strictly speaking, personal, social, or racial, but economic;[1] and this fact must not be lost sight of in any such study.

Housing congestion in our large industrial centers is not wrought by the habits or standards of living of immigrants, but is forced upon them by conditions not of their own choosing or making, such as low wages, high rents, poor city planning, inadequate building laws, and the notorious neglect on the part of city administrations of so-called "foreign" sections.[2] "That bad housing conditions are not the exclusive characteristic of the immigrant, but are found under like economic conditions among the native wage-earners as well, has been shown by the investigation of the Immigration Commission in Alabama, where there are practically no foreigners

[1] Jenks, p. 117.
[2] Hourwich, pp. 235-240.

whose competition might be supposed to have forced down the American standard of living, and where 'the home of the native white laborer is frequently devoid of the more modern equipment and sanitation.' ''[3] And in southern mill-towns, where the mill-workers are largely country people of old American stock, the company houses in which they live "are neither sheathed, plastered, nor papered, and the tenants suffer intensely from occasional cold weather."[4]

In judging the Poles, then, we must take into account their wages and the housing conditions in America as they find them. In the households investigated by the Immigration Commission the average number of persons per 100 rooms was only 134, and per 100 sleeping rooms 232. The Poles averaged per 100 rooms 155 persons, while the Slovenians averaged 172 persons per 100 rooms and South Italians 166 persons. When the average number of persons per sleeping room is taken, the Poles average 2.72 persons per sleeping room, the Slovenians—2.99, the South Italians—2.54, the Magyars—2.43, as compared with an average of 2.03 among Germans and 1.93 among native Americans.[5]

Overcrowding is most frequently shown by the keeping of boarders or lodgers. Among the native Americans 10.2% of the families keep boarders; among the foreign-born—27.2%. Among the foreign-born the Poles occupy the sixth place with 35.5% of the Polish families keeping boarders or lodgers, the Lithuanians leading with 70.2%; then follow the Hungarians with 47.3%, North Italians—42.9%, Swedes—37.2%, and Slovaks with 41%.[6]

[3] Hourwich, p. 246; see also Reports of the Immigration Commission, IX, 229.
[4] Streightoff, Standard of Living, p. 92; Hourwich, p. 246; Jenks, p. 279.
[5] Jenks, pp. 119-120.
[6] Ibidem, p. 121.

The household of immigrants, as compared with the native-born wage-earners, pays, generally speaking, the same, if not higher rent per room, but lower rent per person, as among the immigrants, there is, generally speaking, a much larger number of persons per room. The native-born white pays $2.51 on the average per room per month, while the foreign-born pays $2.90. The native-born, then, with a much higher income pays less rent per room per month than the foreign-born with a decidedly smaller income is required to pay. That under such conditions congestion is inevitable is perfectly clear. Of the foreign-born the South Italians pay $3.28 per room per month, the Slovenians $2.20, the Russian Jews $3.51. The Greeks pay the highest average per room, $4.59, and the Poles the lowest, $1.60. The lowest rent per person is paid by the immigrant Slovenian, $1.29; next ranks the immigrant Pole, $1.34; the Pole of foreign father, but native-born pays $1.35; the Slovak pays $1.37; the South Italian $1.91; and the Russian Jew $2.33. These rents are, of course, pre-war and not post-war rents. In all these cases it is perfectly clear that the effort is made to reduce rent per person by increasing the number of persons per room, i. e., by taking on boarders or lodgers, which low wages and high rents make inevitable.[7]

Of the families studied by the Immigration Commission one-tenth own their homes. Of the native-born families 5.7% own their homes, and of the foreign-born 10.4%. Among the immigrants, 25.8% of the Germans own their homes; of the Swedes 19.4%; of the Poles 17%; of the Irish 12.5%; and of the Slovenians 11.1%.[8] These percentages, however, have been greatly modified in the course of the last few years in favor of larger home-ownership among

[7] Jenks, p. 122.
[8] Ibidem, p. 123.

all groups. Among the Poles, for instance, it is safe to say, that 75% of the Polish families own their homes at the present time, 1921.

The degree of house cleanliness among the Poles is noteworthy. Miss Janet E. Kemp in her Report on Housing Conditions in Baltimore says: "Of the four districts investigated, the Thames Street district—which, by the way, is the worst housing district in the Polish section of Baltimore—ranks first in the matter of interior cleanliness. Of its 904 rooms, 808 were described as clean, and out of 322 halls and stairways only 32, or slightly less than 10%, were found to be dirty. Throughout the investigation no impossibly high standard of cleanliness was applied. All rooms, halls, yards, and cellars that were not positively dirty were classed as clean. But in the Thames Street district, in nearly all cases, the adjective may be considered as descriptive of actual conditions. A remembered Saturday evening inspection of five apartments in a house in Thames Street, with their whitened floors and shining cook stoves, with the dishes gleaming on the neatly ordered shelves, the piles of clean clothing laid out for Sunday, and the general atmosphere of preparation for the Sabbath, suggested standards that would not have disgraced a Puritan housekeeper."

Family life.—The family is regarded with respect and reverence. Family life is still largely of the patriarchal type; the father is the undisputed nominal, though not always real, head of the family. The mother occupies, in theory at least, but not necessarily in practice, a somewhat secondary place, and the children are trained in filial respect and obedience. Polish families, as a rule, are large, with an average of five to six children to the family.[9] The family forms an economic unit. In many instances

[9] Jenks, p. 61.

the labor of the wife and the children supplements that of the husband and father. The earnings of the family go into a common treasury, and are distributed to each member according to his or her needs. Of course, as the economic condition of the family improves, the mother is relieved of outside work, devoting her entire attention to the home and the family, and the children are given an opportunity to secure better education. The standard of morality is, on the whole, high among the Poles. An evidence of this is found in the vigor and vitality of the Polish stock and in the small number of divorces among the Polish people. Owing to a difference in language, customs, ideas, and the general American environment, parental authority and influence is not infrequently lessened, and the second generation is apt to grow up quite independent of home influences, which does not always result in a better type of manhood and womanhood and in a more desirable citizenship. On the whole, however, the second generation of Polish immigrants makes as good citizens as any other national group produces; and these ''as a rule adopt the language and the customs of the country.'' [10]

Intermarriage.—Intermarriage between the Poles and other nationalities plays as yet a very small rôle. According to the Census of 1910 97.2% of Polish immigrant families were nationally homogeneous, with both parents born in Poland, and only 2.8% were mixed, with one parent born in Poland and one native. And even in the case of the 2.8% mixed marriages the fact must not be lost sight of that many a parent recorded as native was of Polish nationality born in this country. It is also interesting to note that more Polish-born men marry native-born women (2.2%) than native-born men marry Polish-born women (0.5%); and that the percentage

[10] Kruszka, I, p. 87.

of women born in other foreign countries married
to Polish-born men is slightly larger than that of
native-born women, 2.9% as to 2.2%.[11]

Relation to native Americans.—It is a well-known
fact that the native American population does not
stay in the sections of our cities invaded by immigrants, but moves to up-town districts or to the
suburbs. Those that actually do remain for business or other reasons constitute a very small and
scattered group. This naturally leaves the immigrant settlements solidly foreign and quite to themselves. It certainly is true of the Polish settlements,
especially of the larger ones in our larger city-
centers. Quite naturally, too, there is no social intercourse between the Poles and the Americans, and
very little, if any, between the Poles and other immigrant groups for the same reason. Whatever
intercourse there exists between the Poles and the
Americans, is of a business or political, but not of
a social nature. This sharp line of social demarca-
tion has tended to preserve and to perpetuate a dis-
tinctly foreign character of our city immigrant communities by natural and inevitable necessity. We
learn and assimilate by contact; where there is no
contact, there is no exchange of ideas and no assimilation. However, the feeling of the Poles toward
the native Americans is cordial, and in as far as
they have opportunity to become acquainted with
what is best in American social life, they readily
make it their own.

Social life and recreation.—Being left to themselves, the Polish immigrant communities have by
necessity had to preserve and develop a social life
and forms of recreation of their own. The Pole's
intense social and hospitable nature finds expression, pleasure, and satisfaction in frequent "getting
together." The Pole likes to visit, to talk, to en-

[11] U. S. Census for 1910.

tertain, and to have a good time. He passionately loves music, dancing, and dramatic art. Weddings and christenings furnish great opportunities for sociability; holidays are taken advantage of for social visiting, and in summer for family picnics; musical concerts and dramatic plays always find favor with the Poles, and, if good, are thoroughly enjoyed and appreciated. In anteprohibition days the saloon was a very popular social and recreational center; but now the home, friends, wholesome community entertainments, and the great outdoors receive more attention, and furnish sociability and recreation.

Civic life and political relations.—At first for a number of years the Poles took small part in civic and political affairs; but their interest and participation in them have been growing rapidly in recent years. With improvement in their economic condition and with greater acquisition of property and of the English language as well, their interest in civic and political matters has been aroused, and as a result a greater percentage of them have become naturalized citizens. Of the Poles studied by the Immigration Commission that have been in the United States from 5 to 9 years 33.1% have either been naturalized or hold first papers; of those that have been here 10 years and more, 39.8% have been fully naturalized.[12] This percentage has been considerably raised during the war and since. It may probably be safe to say that at present (1921) 50-60%, if not more, of the Poles in this country are naturalized American citizens.

As to political affiliations, both parties count Poles as members. In the days before the Civil War the slavery issue tended to draw the Poles into the Republican ranks, and many of them fought gallantly on the side of the Union. It is interesting to find, writes Miss Balch, that the Poles voted for Grant

[12] Jenks, pp. 272, 273, 406.

in 1872,—the first election in which they were notably interested,—because he recognized the French Republic during the Prussian War, while his opponent, Greeley, was supposed to favor Austria in Italy and Germany in Alsace-Lorraine.[13] On the other hand, it is claimed that in Chicago Poles are "normally Democrats."[14] In the election of 1920 many supported the Democratic candidate out of gratitude to President Wilson for his stand regarding Poland. Both Republicans and Democrats have nominated Poles to office; and a number of these nominees have been elected and have sat in city councils and in state legislatures, both in the lower chamber and in the upper.[15]

Organizations.—Polish life in the United States is well organized. In 1905 the Poles numbered as many as three to four thousand organizations of various kinds, religious, secular, and mixed. The largest of these is the Polish National Alliance, organized under the present name in 1880, but going under different names as far back as 1842. The purpose of this organization is "to promote the moral and material development of Polish immigrants in the United States through the establishment of Polish 'Homes,' schools, and benevolent institutions, and through the encouragement of Polish industry; to encourage temperance; and to maintain the proper observance of national holidays."[16] In 1904 the Alliance numbered 595 locals with a total membership of 40,035. Between 1886 and 1904, inclusive, it had paid out $1,517,378.95 in death benefits and insurance, and had a balance in its treasury of $242,441.53. At present (1921) it has a membership of 125,000, and maintains a daily and a weekly publica-

[13] Our Slavic Fellow Citizens, pp. 394-395.
[14] Ibidem, p. 395.
[15] Ibidem, p. 395; Kruszka, III, pp. 132-134.
[16] Kruszka, IV, p. 22.

tion, an Immigrant Home in New York City, and a
High School at Cambridge Springs, Pa., and by
means of stipends assists Polish students in their
efforts to acquire a higher education.[17] While nomi-
nally secular and non-sectarian, the Alliance has
been very much under clerical influence in recent
years, very conservative and very reactionary. The
headquarters of the Alliance is in Chicago.

Of next importance is the Polish National Defence Committee known also by its Polish initials as
the K. O. N. This organization came into being several years before the war. Its original purpose was
to promote education among the Polish immigrants
in this country, and to work for Poland's independence. Its spirit and policies have been liberal and
progressive; and the K. O. N. has rallied to itself
all the liberal and progressive element among the
Polish immigrants, regardless of differences in religious, economic, or political views. During the
war the K. O. N. supported General Pilsudski and
his Polish legions, opposed Polish reliance on Russia up to the time of the fall of the Czarist régime,
and advocated a policy of self-reliance and oppor-
tunism. On that account it was very much misun-
derstood and misrepresented and even its loyalty to
this Government was questioned. However, as to
the last there was absolutely no rational ground
whatever for any such suspicion; for the K. O. N.
welcomed the entrance of the United States into the
European War, and built its hopes for Polish independence on it in a large measure. The membership
of the K. O. N. does not approach that of the Alliance, but it represents the more progressive element
among the Poles. The chief object of the organization now is educational. Its headquarters are also
in Chicago.

Besides these two most important organizations

[17] McClure, pp. 70-76.

of opposite extremes, the one conservative and reactionary and the other liberal and progressive,
there are several other organizations of importance
like the Polish Roman Catholic Union, the Polish
Falkans, or "Sokols," the Polish Women's Union,
and the Polish Singers Union of America. These
national organizations are further supplemented by
an innumerable number of local organizations of one
kind or another, in which different phases of Polish
social life and activity center, and find expression.

The Church.—The most important Polish social
institution is the church. It is the first one to be
established, and its centralizing power is beyond
dispute. Around it, and stimulated by it, grows the
Polish colony, with its agencies well organized and
controlled. The church not only expresses the religious aspirations of the Poles and ministers to
their religious needs, but also completely dominates
the entire life of the colony. This accounts for the
unprogressive character of some of the smaller Polish colonies. The larger ones, in which the domi-
nating influence of the church is weaker, show more
independence, activity, and progress.

**Educational institutions: (a) The parochial
school.**—The next most important Polish social institution is the Polish parochial school. This institution owes its origin to the instinct of self-preser-
vation. Deeply religious and nationalistic, the Polish immigrant has striven, not only to worship God
in his mother-tongue, but also to have his children
instructed in his native language. This all the more
so, because under Prussian and Russian rule he had
been forbidden to have his children taught in Polish.
And the clergy, regarding the Polish parochial
school as the very foundation of the Polish Roman
Catholic Church in this country have taken the initiative in its organization and establishment.[18] **To**

[18] Kruszka, II, pp. 83, 84; cf. Balch, p. 416.

determine the number of Polish parochial schools, one must know the approximate number of Polish parishes. This was in 1900 about 500, and in 1910 about 600. The number of children enrolled in these schools in 1901 was approximately 70,000, and the teaching force consisted of 200 secular male teachers and 804 convent sisters, or about one teacher to every 70 children.[19]

The value of the physical equipment of these schools at that time was estimated at six million dollars. The annual salaries paid to teachers amounted to $140,000 for male teachers and $160,000 for sisters, making an annual total of $300,000.[20]

The course of instruction in the Polish parochial schools embraces eight years and is supposed to cover all such subjects as are commonly taught in elementary and grammar grades, with religious instruction added. The work done is regarded as equal to that of the public schools.[21] Moreover, Father Kruszka claims that children going from the Polish parochial schools to public schools enter corresponding classes, and in some instances are actually promoted to higher grades.[22] We have no desire here to controvert Father Kruszka's statements, but we must say that his evaluation of the work of the Polish parochial schools is greatly overstated. To our knowledge the instruction in the Polish parochial schools does not equal that of the public schools, and children going from Polish parochial schools to public schools must, invariably and as a rule, enter lower grades, because of inadequate preparation for the work of corresponding grades, not to speak of advanced grades. In support of this

[19] Kruszka, II, pp. 86-88.
[20] Ibidem, II, p. 89.
[21] Ibidem, II, p. 97.
[22] Ibidem, II, p. 98.

contention we cite a Polish press criticism of Polish parochial schools:—

"Being mostly orthodox Catholics, Polish parents are compelled to send their children to Polish parochial schools. All other schools, especially the public schools, are denounced from the pulpit and in the so-called 'church-press' as 'unchristian, pagan and demoralizing institutions.' Parents sending their children to any other but the parochial school are denounced, threatened, ostracized, even expelled from the church, and their children are persecuted. With the exception of those where the priest is a sincere educator, the parochial schools are poor, many of them very poor, educational institutions. Reading, writing, arithmetic, geography, and history are taught in many of them rather superficially. On the other hand many hours are spent every day in reciting catechism and church formulas, which is called 'teaching religion,' but it is far from being really religion. The result of such poor system of teaching is that the Polish children, after spending six or seven years in the parochial school, can hardly pass an examination for the fifth grade in the public schools—if they want to continue their education in the public schools." [23]

As a matter of fact, it may safely be said that the parochial school, whether Polish, Bohemian, Italian, or any other, is a menace rather than a blessing to the welfare of the immigrants themselves as well as of the nation; for it fails to prepare the immigrant's children adequately for their competitive economic struggle in the new land alongside of those going through the public school and for intelligent participation in civic and political life. Out of consideration, therefore, for the real welfare both of the immigrants and of the nation at large, the parochial school should be done away with. And as to

[23] Balch, App. XXVI, p. 477.

teaching the children of the immigrants their respective mother tongues, that could be provided for
at much less expense by the various immigrant
groups in hours outside of the public school. A new
language is an added avenue leading to the hidden
intellectual and spiritual treasures of a people. The
more such avenues the citizenship of a nation is
familiar with the greater is the national access to
the intellectual and spiritual treasures of others and
the richer that nation's intellectual and spiritual
life. Not suppression of native languages and sentiments among our immigrant groups, but their development and utilization should be our aim. It will
enrich our own culture, enlarge our resourcefulness,
and increase our strength.

(b) The public school.—Owing to the strong national consciousness of the Poles and the presence
of a parochial school in nearly every Polish community of any appreciable size, the feeling prevails
among the Poles and native Americans alike that
the majority of Polish children attend the parochial
schools. Yet on reflection and investigation the interesting fact is revealed that after all the majority
of Polish children of school age are to be found in
the public schools. In his history of the Poles in
America Father Kruszka estimates the number of
children in Polish parochial schools in 1901 at about
70,000. The Polish population in the United States
is estimated to number 3,500,000. Allowing one-
third of this number for surplus male immigrants,
and dividing the remainder by five, the number of
individuals to a family, we obtain 466,733, the number of families. Now, granting that of the three-
fifths of family members two-fifths are children
either above or below school age, we have one-fifth
left, or 466,733, the number of Polish children of
school age, that is, one child of school age in every
family. Taking 70,000 as the average annual num-

ber of Polish children in the parochial schools and deducting it from 466,733, we still have 396,733, or approximately 400,000 Polish children of school age, who obviously can be nowhere else except in the public schools. This calculation finds support in the results of the investigation made by the Immigration Commission. The Commission's report included information for a total of 2,036,376 school children, of whom 221,159, or 9.64% of the total, were in parochial schools. Of those in the public schools 766,727, or 42.2%, were children of native-born fathers, while 1,048,490, or 57.8%, were children of foreign-born fathers. Of these pupils some were born abroad, and some in the United States.[24]

Among the children enumerated in the public schools included in the Commission's report the percentage of retardation was as follows: White children of native-born fathers 34.1%; children of foreign-born parents 36%. The highest percentage of retardation was found among the South Italians, 48.6%; next to them rank the Poles with 48.1%; then come the North Italians with 45.9%; and then the French Canadians with 43.1%. Best of all rank the Finnish children with only 27.7% retardation; then the Swedish with 28.7%; the Dutch with 31.1%; the Welsh with 32%; the English with 33.7%; and the Norwegian with 33.9%.[25] This makes it perfectly evident that the children of Catholic parents are the ones that show the highest percentage of retardation, while children of Protestant parents show the lowest percentage of retardation!

(c) **Secondary schools.**—The Polish elementary parochial schools are supplemented by several secondary institutions such as the College of the Resurrectionist Fathers in Chicago, the Polish National Alliance High School at Cambridge Springs, Pa., a

[24] Jenks, pp. 282, 283.
[25] Ibidem, p. 286.

A GROUP OF POLISH WOMEN IN AGRICULTURE. (U.S.)

A GROUP OF POLISH MEN IN AGRICULTURE. (U.S.)

[See page 73

YOUNG POLISH MINERS (U.S.)

LEARNING ENGLISH IN THE FORD SHOPS DETROIT

[See p(

School for Women of the Holy Family in Philadelphia, Pa., a Polish Theological Seminary at Orchard Lake, Michigan, and others.[26] These institutions, however, do not draw any appreciable number of Polish youth. Polish young men and young women seeking higher education prefer to go to American high schools, colleges, and universities.

(d) Night schools.—Another educational force is night schools, public and private. Their importance as an educational factor in Polish communities must not be underestimated. They serve the adults and young people above school age. Many a Polish immigrant has here acquired a knowledge of English, or has laid a foundation for further study. For many the night school has been a door opening on a wide vista of opportunity, and leading to success in the new land. But for the night school many a one would be deprived of an opportunity for self-improvement, and the country of a more useful and valuable citizen. The influence of night schools in foreign communities is unquestionably great.

(e) Lecture courses.—Still another potent educational force have been the so-called ''Uniwersytety ludowe,'' or popular lecture courses arranged for and offered to the public either by some organization or by a group of public-spirited men and women interested in the social and educational welfare of their countrymen. Such popular lecture courses have been established and are maintained in many of the larger Polish centers. The lectures cover a wide range of subjects, vary from year to year, and are of great educational and spiritual value.

(f) Polish National Halls.—Then, too, we must not fail to mention the Polish National Halls as educational institutions and forces. These are Polish ''Community Buildings,'' erected and operated as Polish community centers by the Polish citizens or-

[26] Okolowicz, p. 51.

ganized as stock companies or corporations. There is scarcely a Polish settlement of any size without such a "hall," or "home." And these halls constitute the centers of Polish organized life and of Polish educational and social activities. To be sure, in some places, in pre-prohibition times, these National Halls were only common ordinary saloons and dance-halls. In other places, where the clerical influence predominates, they have been converted into church halls. But in most places they have preserved their original purpose and have been centers for good along the line of educational and social activities and life.

Polish press.—At the outbreak of the World War the Polish periodical press in the United States was composed of fifteen dailies and sixty weeklies. Since then several more dailies, weeklies, and monthlies have sprung into being, so that it may be safe to say that the present total number of Polish periodical publications is not far from a hundred. These are published chiefly in the larger Polish centers like Milwaukee, Chicago, Detroit, Toledo, Cleveland, Buffalo, Boston, New York, Philadelphia, Baltimore, and Pittsburgh, although many a smaller place is not without a local weekly.

The oldest Polish weekly publication is the "Zgoda," founded in 1878 in Milwaukee, and in 1888 transferred to Chicago. The "Zgoda" is the official organ of the Polish National Alliance. The oldest Polish daily in the United States is the "Kurjer Polski," founded in 1888 in Milwaukee by Michael Kruszka.[27]

The circulation of the seventy-five Polish publications totaled 1,238,418 at the outbreak of the war; the present total circulation is doubtless larger. The circulation of the Polish dailies runs from 5,000 to 30,000, and of the weeklies from 5,000 to 120,000

[27] Okolowicz, p. 59.

copies. In this connection the thing worthy of note is the fact that the liberal and progressive publications, of anti-clerical tendencies, have a larger circulation than the conservative and clerical. For instance, the "Kurjer Polski," a radical and anti-clerical daily, published in Milwaukee, has a circulation of 20,000 copies, whereas the "Nowiny Polskie," a clerical daily, published in that city, has a circulation of only 10,000 copies. In Detroit the liberal daily, "Kurjer Polski," is reported to have a circulation of 15,000, and the conservative "Rekord Codzienny" only 8,000 copies. In Buffalo the conservative clerical daily, "Polak w Ameryce," reports a circulation of 6,000, and the liberal "Dziennik dla Wszystkich"—a daily circulation of 16,000 copies. And the "Ameryka-Echo," a liberal and distinctively anti-clerical weekly, published in Toledo, Ohio, has a circulation of 80,000 copies, and is probably the most widely read paper of any Polish publication in the United States. The "Zgoda" reports a circulation of 120,000; but it is not a subscription publication; it is the official organ of the Polish National Alliance, sent to every member of the organization, and such publications are seldom diligently read.[28] It is interesting to note also that nearly all of the foreign language editors agree that their papers are not read by the young people, but mainly by the old.[29]

As to quality the Polish American press is not of a high order; yet, on the whole, it compares favorably with similar publications in other languages, and still more so when it is remembered that it is the material and intellectual product of the Polish peasant immigrant.

Leadership.—The leadership among the Polish immigrants in America is in the hands of the ex-

---

[28] Okolowicz, pp. 59-60.
[29] McClure, p. 39.

saloon-keepers, the priests, a select number of well educated immigrant Poles, and the rising generation of Polish Americans brought up in the American atmosphere and trained in our American institutions. The first two groups of leaders, the ex-saloon-keepers and the priests, are usually found to work together hand-in-glove; for both groups are exploiters of the people and social parasites, with no ideas to advance, but to prey on the masses. They are naturally reliable conservatives. The other two groups divide into conservatives and progressives according to their primary object in life. Those whose chief ambition is to make a quick success in business or profession rather than to be concerned about the general welfare of society usually line up with the conservatives, the ex-saloon-keepers and the priests, the men of influence and authority. Those, on the other hand, whose dominant desire in life is to contribute something to the sum total of social well-being, to advance ideas and to promote social welfare, regardless of material success, as a rule tear loose, and line up with the progressives. Among the organized agencies the leadership is divided between the Polish National Alliance and the Polish Defence Committee or K. O. N.; the Alliance representing the ultra-conservative and reactionary elements and the K. O. N. leading the liberals and, generally speaking, the forces of progress.

Assimilation.—The early Polish immigrants, patriots and men of education, melted into the common life so completely that the later comers could find no point of attachment with them. The more recent immigrants have come in much larger numbers; they have formed solid colonies; and as an inevitable consequence they have in a remarkable degree preserved their language and their distinctive customs. On the other hand, all efforts in the direction of preservation of racial and national distinctions are as nothing against the irresistible influence of environment and of American-born children. Parents may be surprised, proud, or scandalized, but they are powerless to prevent the transforming process. The influence of environment and the innate positive dislike of children to be different from their playmates are very potent forces in the Americanization of the second generation. Americanization, however, does not necessarily mean a denial or a refusal to learn one's native tongue. This should be encouraged rather than discouraged for reasons of parental home discipline, of leadership among newcomers, and of national welfare and strength in emergencies.[30] "It is right enough that the immigrant into an English-speaking nation should learn the English language. But, on the other hand, it is altogether desirable that Americans should broaden their own culture by learning from the immigrant as well as by teaching him. In no other way can the possible benefits of the amalgamation of national and racial types be secured. We quite rightly ask them to abandon their old loyalties; but we shall be incredibly foolish if we also constrain them to forget the culture they have inherited. We blame our foreigners for their clannishness. We resent the fact that they sequester themselves among people of their own race, and do not take the trouble to understand our language or our history and institutions; but we are guilty of an analogous piece of provincialism when we betray our unwillingness to learn from them, while expecting them to learn from us. The Pole usually knows Russian and German, and even French, as well as his native tongue. In Switzerland one can hardly find a schoolboy who has not three languages in tolerable repair and in constant use."[31] A knowl-

[30] See Balch, pp. 412-416.
[31] See Bridges, pp. 56-61.

edge of more than one language means so many mas-
ter-keys to the intellectual and spiritual treasures
of more than one literature. With her citizenship
drawn from the ends of the earth, no country has a
more magnificent opportunity to be the proud mis-
tress of the languages and the literatures of the
world than the United States. And yet no country
in the world can possibly be as blind to any opportunity as we are to this unsurpassed opportunity
of ours!

But it is not only the second generation of Polish
immigrants that becomes rapidly assimilated. The
first generation, too, is fairly responsive to the influence of its new environment. Among the employees in the packing houses of Kansas City, the
Immigration Commission found that while of the
German employees under 5 and 9 and over 10 years
in the United States only 20%, 70%, and 95.8% respectively could speak English, the percentages of
Polish employees speaking English were 26.1%,
73.2%, and 100% for corresponding periods of residence in the United States.[32] In the clothing industry, taking the same periods of residence in this
country, the percentages for male Bohemian and
Moravian employees speaking English were 22.5%,
45.0%, and 75.0%, and for female employees of the
same nationality—18.1%, 57.5%, and 88.0% respectively; for male Polish employees the percentages
were 24.8%, 62.4%, and 83.2%, and for Polish female employees they were 19.4%, 63.0%, and 89.4%
respectively.[33] Of the total Polish immigrant population of both sexes 39.1% speak English.[34] Moreover, an evidence of Polish Americanism and of Polish loyalty to the Government of the United States
is the ready participation of the Poles in all the wars

[32] Hourwich, p. 78; Reports, Vol. 13, Table 256, p. 329.
[33] Ibidem, p. 58; Reports, Vol. II, p. 363, Table 95.
[34] Jenks, pp. 407-409.

of the Union, from the Revolutionary War down to the Great World War.[35] On our entrance into the World War President Wilson called for 100,000 volunteers; 40,000 of those responding were Poles. In view of the fact that they make up only 3.18% of our population it is very significant that during the War there were 220,000 Poles in the United States Army; that on the casualty lists 10% are Polish names; that of the peoples of foreign birth or descent they are rated fourth in their contributions to the Liberty Loans with $67,000,000.[36]

[35] Kruszka, III, p. 134-136; IV, pp. 10-12.
[36] Rev. D. G. Jaxheimer, Ms. on the Poles.

CHAPTER V: RELIGIOUS CONDITIONS

RELIGIOUS CONDITIONS

OUTSTANDING CHARACTERISTICS

Religion of the Poles.—In religion the Poles are predominantly Roman Catholic. Their devotion to the Church of Rome, as a result of temperamental and historical conditions, surpasses that of any other nationality.[1] The Protestants constitute only 6.6% of the total Polish population, and their number among Polish immigrants in the U. S. is very small and scattered.

The Poles are a very religious people, possessed of a deep religious instinct and a temperament particularly susceptible to religious impressions. Religion permeates the Polish peasant's thought, speech, and daily life. The names of Christ and the Virgin are on his lips all the time. His legends and folklore are religious in character. His patriotism and his religion are inseparably linked together in his mind. A good Pole is expected to be a good Catholic. A testimony to the religious fervor of the Poles is their many sanctuaries, cathedrals, and shrines in the homeland and their churches in this country. The Poles have always been very liberal in their gifts to religion; hence their church edifices usually are large, highly ornamented, not infrequently imposing, and often charming. Their worship is full of imagery, pageantry, and symbolism. Their devotion is intense. It is almost pitiful

[1] Cf. Winter, p. 274.

—says Winter—the desperation with which the Polish peasants cling to what seems to a Westerner to be antiquated religious forms, and into the observance of which they seem to throw their whole soul. The men in the churches equal the women in numbers, and they seem fully as absorbed in their devotion.[2]

Pilgrimages are common and popular. Czenstochowa, a town midway between Warsaw and Cracow, is the Mecca of the Poles. Here is the home of the "Mother of God of Czenstochowa," the Queen and Protectress of Poland. Her sacred picture, reported to have been drawn by St. Luke upon the cypress table top from the Nazareth home, forms the altar-piece of a small chapel in the cathedral.[3] This place is the central point of Polish religious history. The Poles consider it a great privilege to be permitted to make a pilgrimage to Czenstochowa. No sacrifice is too great to be made in order to accomplish the journey. Bands of pilgrims are almost constantly coming in from some direction. Sometimes hundreds and even thousands of peasants may be seen lying flat on their faces during worship, each one muttering his prayers. In places the stones are actually worn by the contact of the knees of the worshipers. Before Poland's partitions it was the custom even for the royal processions on the way from Warsaw to Cracow for the coronation ceremonies to stop at this shrine.[4]

Children are early taught to say their prayers and to perform the various acts of homage. The sacred images in the churches are worn smooth by the osculations of the devoted worshipers. Every conceivable device is employed by the clergy to obtain and retain control of the simple mind of the peasant.

[2] Cf. Winter, pp. 275-276.
[3] Hayden, p. 13.
[4] Cf. Winter, pp. 277, 279.

Every material that can draw the attention of the eye, and every sound that will attract the ear, is employed in the religious symbols.[5]

The religion of the Poles is chiefly a religion of external rites, symbolic forms, servile fear, and magical personal salvation rather than of spiritual idealism and inner freedom, filial trust and loving obedience, purity of heart and outward moral conduct, practical brotherly love and social service. It rests on ignorance instead of on intelligence. It appeals to superstition instead of to rational moral and social idealism. While the religious temperament and the deeply religious nature of the Poles are of priceless value, and furnish a solid rock-bottom foundation for a magnificent superstructure of real, vital, and practical personal and social religion, the actual religious superstructure erected upon this wonderful foundation has been rather valueless. Its external form and decorations are, to be sure, almost literally of gold, silver, and precious stones; but its internal frame-work and substance are, unfortunately, too much of wood, hay, and stubble. It is, therefore, largely useless, a showy but burdensome liability, a serious obstacle in the way of individual, social, and national progress and development.

This is the religious heritage the Polish peasant immigrants bring with them. True to the example of the patriarchs of old, the early discoverers and explorers of this continent, and the Pilgrim Fathers of later days, who, when they came to a new country, first of all built an altar to Jehovah, raised the cross, or erected a meeting house to the honor and glory of their God, the Poles, on their arrival in this country, just as soon as a sufficient number of them has settled in a place, build their church in which they may worship God according to the cus-

[5] Cf. Winter, p. 277.

toms of their fathers in the homeland. The Polish
settlement grows around the church, which is the
center of its life and activity.

In 1900, according to Father Kruszka, the Poles in
this country had 520 churches and 550 priests.[6] By
1910 the number of Polish churches increased to
about 600 and that of priests to about 1,000.[7] Since
then, owing to the War and the stoppage of immigration, the growth, if any, in the number of churches
has been insignificant. Some of the Polish churches
are of considerable size and beauty; they are struc-
tures which, according to Dr. Steiner, might well be
the pride of any community, or, according to Mr.
Okolowicz, a notable adornment of any European
capital.[8] On Sundays and on other church holidays
as well, these churches are filled with worshipers to
overflowing; for the Poles are a church-going people.

Disintegrating forces.—Our free, critical, inquiring, and extremely practical American atmosphere,
however, has a disintegrating influence upon their
religion. Nor can it be otherwise. A religion of
external forms, however elaborate, over-awing, or
charming these may be, based on ignorance, super-
sition, and fear, cannot hold its ground.[9] Sooner
or later it is bound to fall a prey to inevitable disintegration and decay. This process of religious disintegration is more rapid in its operation in some
cases than in others. Among the Czechs and Italians, for instance, it is decidedly more rapid than
among the Poles.

The slower disintegration of religious faith and
forms among the Poles is due to several causes.
First, as has already been noted, the Polish peasant
possesses a deeply religious nature and is very

[6] Vol. I, p. 88.
[7] Okolowicz, p. 50.
[8] Cf. Dr. Steiner, On the Trail, p. 211, and Okolowicz, p. 50.
[9] Cf. McClure, pp. 78-79.

loyal. He is not much inclined to scepticism, nor
to change of loyalty. He is generous and true; he
trusts implicitly, is devotedly loyal, and may, in
turn, be fully depended upon. He is neither the
first nor the last either to accept a new thing and
pin his faith to it, or to give up readily an old tried
thing. He prefers to pursue a safe middle course.
It may take him longer to give up an old worn-out
idea or institution and to take up with something
new; but when he once does a thing wholeheartedly,
his faith and loyalty may be depended upon. Secondly, the Roman Catholic Church has remarkably
well succeeded in persuading the Polish peasant to
believe that his national fortunes are inseparably
tied up with Roman Catholicism. This, of course,
is not true, as history plainly shows; yet it is generally believed to be true, and the belief is not altogether without some historical foundation. Poland's
most implacable enemies and oppressors, Russia
and Germany, are of different religious faiths, Russian Orthodox and Protestant. The portion of divided Poland in which the Poles enjoyed the largest
measure of autonomy and liberty before the Restoration was not the Congress [10] Kingdom under the
rule of Orthodox Russia, nor Posen under the rule
of Protestant Germany, but Galicia under the rule
of Catholic Austria. Even today the best conti-
nental friend of Poland is Catholic France rather
than Protestant England. In the light of these
facts, it is not to be wondered at that it has been
so easy for the Roman Catholic Church to foist on
the Poles the belief in the identity of their nationality with Roman Catholicism. Polish strong patriotism, therefore, has naturally dictated at least
nominal adherence and conformity to the established national church. And, thirdly, social consid-

[10] A kingdom, with the Czar as king, constituted by the Congress
of Vienna in 1815, out of the remnant of Poland.

erations, too, tend to preserve and maintain this outward religious conformity. The operation of these causes explains, in a large measure, the slower disintegration of religion and its forms among the Poles as compared with conditions among other nationalities.

But while the causes just described have retarded the disintegrating process of traditional religion among the Poles, they have not prevented it. The ecclesiastical and religious disintegration has been in force; and it has been greatly stimulated by the influence of our free political and social institutions, the separation of Church and State in this country, our great variety of religious denominations, and our friendly harmonious life in spite of many differences of opinion, belief, profession, and political as well as religious affiliation. Its results are significant. It is variously estimated that the number of Poles who have broken away from the Roman Catholic Church embraces from one-fifth to one-third of the total Polish immigrant population in the United States.[11]

Forms of religious break-up.—The ecclesiastical and religious break-up among the Poles is taking on the forms (1) of religious doubt, apathy, and growing religious indifference; (2) of open revolt against the domineering and dictatorial attitude of the hierarchy of the Church; and (3) of actual hostility and undisguised opposition, not only to the Church of Rome, but to all churches and to religion as well. The last-named form of religious break-up does not assume any significant proportions among the Poles,[12] although here and there its influence appears to be considerably strong and active. The reason for that is to be found in the deeply religious

---

[11] Father Kruszka estimates it at one-third; McClure at one-fifth.
[12] See McClure, p. 79.

nature of the Poles. Cases of open group-revolt
against the autocracy of the hierarchy of the Church
are not infrequent;[13] and in many instances they
have resulted in an out-and-out break with the
Church of Rome. Wherever this occurs, it is a result of the Pole's natural and intense love of liberty
coming to the fore and asserting itself in religion no
less than in politics.[14] Those that are under the
influence of religious doubt, apathy, or of out-and-
out indifference are the most numerous and constitute the largest group.

**Forms of religious re-alignment. (a) The Polish
National Independent Catholic Church.**—In nature
every chemical decomposition leads to new chemical
combinations, and to the development of new forms.
It is, therefore, of great interest to know the new religious alignments among the Poles. Wherever there
occurs a complete group-break with the Church of
Rome, as a result of some abuses on the part of the
Roman hierarchy, it most frequently leads to the
formation of a Catholic church independent of the
Roman organization. In this way the Polish National Independent Catholic Church arose with
Bishop Francis Hodur, of Scranton, Pa., as its organizer, leader, and head. The movement is largely
a protest against the domination of the Polish Roman Catholic Church in this country by Irish and
Roman Catholic groups and a demand for parish
control of church-property. It numbers about 50
churches, most of which are in the State of Penn-
sylvania; it has a benefit "Union," with 72 local
branches; and it publishes a weekly paper, which is
its official organ, and which purports to reach a
constituency of about 50,000 readers. In faith and
worship the Polish National Church is still Catholic;
it retains the Catholic creeds, the mass, the confes-

[13] Cf. McClure, pp. 79-80.
[14] Cf. Ibidem, p. 79.

sional, images, the worship of the Virgin and the saints, and the Roman Church calendar of Holy days. It differs from the Roman Church, however, in the substitution of the Polish language for the Latin in the mass; leaving the matter of auricular confession to the discretion of the individual local priests; giving its members the Scriptures and encouraging them to read it; in the tendency toward a married clergy; and in the matter of a more democratic church administration. The movement marks a step in the right direction. Its chief handicap is a painful lack of the right sort of leadership. If Bishop Hodur had men of good character, religious convictions, high ideals, and proper training, the movement would be making considerable progress.[15]

(b) The Polish Catholic Church of America.—Another very similar religious organization is the Polish Catholic Church in America, with Bishop Francis J. Mazur, of Detroit, Mich., as its organizer and leader. Its rise is to be traced to very much the same causes that led to the organization of the Polish National Church, with this difference that the Polish Catholic Church of America is a protest against both former church organizations, the Roman and the National, that in its administration it is much more democratic than either. Its creed is very progressive, its outlook very broad, and its conception of the Church's social mission quite advanced.

(c) Anti-Church organizations.—Those who have lost faith, not only in the Church, but also in religion, affiliate, in certain instances, with radical organizations, the attitude of which is that of opposition to arbitrary power, and its abuses wherever these appear, whether in politics, industry, or religion. The number of Poles, however, in the ranks

[15] See Hayden, pp. 24-28; McClure, pp. 81-83; and Okolowicz, p. 50.

of the Socialist Party, in the organization of the Industrial Workers of the World, and in other similar organizations, is rather small. The Poles, as we have seen, do not take readily to radicalism of any kind, although, it must be admitted, that tendency is gradually growing stronger. If it is allowed to gather momentum, it will be unfortunate all around; for whatever the Pole does, when he has been fully aroused to action, he does it whole-heartedly, and is apt to go the limit.

(d) **Protestant Churches.**—Those occupying a sort of half-way ground religiously constitute by far the largest group. Estranged from the Roman Catholic Church, and slowly drifting farther and farther away from it, carried by the gentle waves of religious doubt, apathy, and indifference, some are actually finding their way into Protestantism as a result of missionary efforts. The Protestant Churches of America came early to realize the decay in the new environment of the inherited form of religion of many of the immigrant groups. In consequence thereof they have strongly felt it to be their Christian and patriotic duty to meet these people with a new conception and interpretation of the Christian religion and of its place and function in the life of the individual and of organized society. Thus as early as the eighties of the last century some of the Protestant denominations started missionary work among the Polish immigrants, and have been prosecuting it ever since with varying success. According to denominational statistics for 1920, the Baptists report 17 churches and missions, 809 communicant members, 2,000 adherents, 16 Sunday-schools with an enrollment of 580 scholars, and a Training School for Christian workers in East Orange, N. J.; the Methodists—6 churches with a communicant membership of 180, and four Sunday-schools with an enrollment of 258; the Episcopalians

—4 churches, 378 communicants and 546 adherents; the Congregationalist—one church of about sixty communicant members and a fine Sunday-school; and the Presbyterians—3 churches and missions with 140 communicant members and about 1,200 adherents, and 3 church-schools with an enrollment of nearly 500 children.[16] Some of the Poles have come under the direct influence of English-speaking Protestant churches, and have united with them. Others have attached themselves to undenominational organizations, like the Chicago Tract Society, the Y. M. C. A. and the Y. W. C. A.

These figures, however, do not appear to indicate a very strong movement among the religiously drifting Poles toward Protestantism. The situation requires explanation. First, everyone, of course, knows that the statistics cited above do not tell the whole story. They do not register the many Poles who come under Protestant influence, thoroughly appreciate its religious spirit, its moral idealism, and its practical Christian life, but for patriotic, social, and business reasons do not unite with any Protestant church as communicant members. Secondly, every period, it must be borne in mind, of decay and reconstruction, whether in political, economic, or in religious thought, life, and organization, is marked by chaos—by uncertainty and hesitation. There is no instant and direct transformation of the old into the new. When the old has fallen under the stress of inevitable elemental forces, the ground must be cleared first before a new and better structure can be raised, and the clearing of the ground requires labor and time. Most of the present work is of the nature of clearing the ground of the débris and wreckage of the old, of digging deep below the surface through the accumulated errors and prejudices of years, even centuries,

[16] See Denominational Year-Books.

to the rock bottom of the human soul, and of first laying a new and sure foundation of religious thought, upon which in time the superstructure of new religious life and organization may rise in a more beautiful form. This kind of reconstruction work is necessarily slow, inconspicuous, and not easily tabulated. Thirdly, it must be frankly admitted, the Protestant denominations have not taken their religious opportunity among the Poles seriously enough to make the work really effective. They have dealt with it in a haphazard, happy-go-lucky way, without any definite policy or plan for prosecution of the work and without that faith which makes great resources of means, energy, and power available for the removal of mountains of difficulties.

Forms of religious approach.—The religious approach of the Protestant Churches to the Poles, in so far as there has been any definite approach, has taken on the forms of (1) distribution of religious literature, (2) gospel preaching or evangelism, and (3) institutional church work. The first two have been used generally, the third—very little. The social settlement form of approach has not been employed in the Polish work by any Protestant denomination.

The two forms of religious approach most widely used, namely, distribution of religious literature and gospel preaching, are good and perfectly orthodox; their adaptation or application, however, by the users to the work among the Poles has not been particularly happy, nor specially fruitful of results. This has been due to the fact that the American Protestant Churches have labored under a misconception of the real character of the Polish people open to their ministry, and of their most immediate needs. Now, the business of every good mechanic, someone has said, is to know, first, what he is to do, secondly, the material at hand, then he will know what tools to select to convert his material into the desired object. The Protestant Churches, engaged in ministry to the Poles, have reasonably well known what they wanted to do, but they have not sufficiently well understood the nature of the material at hand; hence their tools, or methods of approach, have not always been happily selected, nor skilfully adapted to the purpose in view.

The material has been new, strange, rough and in a measure even uncouth in appearance. The American Churches have naturally been led to think that it was of the poorest sort, and that any common ordinary tools put in the hands of any ordinary workman that was only willing to work would answer. The simplest kind of tract literature has been selected and distributed; preaching has been conducted on the street, or in some abandoned unattractive store room; men have often been employed to do this kind of work without any adequate qualifications, natural or scholastic, for leadership. The methods of approach and the means employed have been determined and shaped by the unfortunate misconception, so strongly prevalent among Americans, that the people to be dealt with are of the lowest grade, intellectually, morally, and spiritually. As a matter of fact, the ignorant, unreasoning, credulous class of Poles is not the class of people that Protestantism can do anything for, or has any responsibility for at this time. These people are perfectly contented in the Roman Catholic Church, they are staunchly loyal to it, they are inaccessible to Protestant influence. To disturb them would be neither wise, nor profitable. Besides, the American Protestant Churches are not desirous of drawing any contented and loyal members of the Roman Catholic Church away from it. They believe in comity, peace, and harmony. The Poles open and accessible to Protestant influence and ministry are the more intelligent and thoughtful class of people, the people who read and think for themselves, and even dare question the status quo of such a sacred institution as the church and its function in organized society. They are the ones that are loose and adrift. To these the Protestant Churches can be a religious guide and interpreter, leading them to the discovery of a new, deeper, broader, and surer religious foundation, to a new, vital, liberating, and invigorating religious experience, and to a higher, more rational, and more practical conception of religion.

But this class of people can neither be reached nor adequately helped by the kind of religious literature we have been placing in their hands, by our street preaching, by our store missions any more than the same wide-awake, restless, thinking, doubting, questioning class of native Americans can be reached by such means or by similar methods. It may even be seriously questioned whether this class of people can be reached and helped by preaching alone. A practical demonstration of religion and Christianity along the line of economic justice, square dealing, neighborliness, ordinary friendliness, and Christian social helpfulness are always more effective. Practical Christian helpfulness, ministering to practical immediate and most keenly felt needs of humanity, paves the way to a higher and more fundamental, though apparently somewhat more abstract, ministry—the ministry to the basic needs of the human spirit. Jesus understood this perfectly well. We are too much inclined to think of him as a preacher. But he was primarily a minister—a friendly and brotherly minister, going about doing good. He healed the sick, fed the hungry, comforted the sorrowful, and thus by this practical friendly ministry to the immediate needs of men and women and children he led the people to a realization of their more hidden needs, to an appreciation of his teaching concerning the divine life he was an example of, and to an awakened desire to make that life their own. This practical ministry to the more immediate needs of the immigrants has not been very popular with our American Protestant Churches, because it has not seemed to be sufficiently spiritual. Institutional church work and social settlement work have been regarded as doubtful methods of approach. Sunday-school work, distribution of religious literature, and preaching have been chiefly relied upon as the only proper methods of religious approach to the immigrants. But even these have not, unfortunately, been scaled up, in the case of the Poles at least, to the spiritual needs of the people.

Thus, the forms of religious approach to the Poles heretofore used have been weak in two points as a result of an under-estimation on the part of the Churches of the value and importance of social service work as well as of the character of the Poles open to Protestant ministry. If, in the future, the Protestant Churches are to make better use of their opportunity among the religiously restless Poles, they must modify their forms of approach in favor of (1) greater use of social service work, (2) more adequate and attractive building-plants, (3) more and better qualified workers, (4) a larger quantity as well as a better quality of Polish religious literature, and (5) a broader, more rational, and more practical interpretation of the Christian religion.

SPECIAL PROBLEMS

The special problems in the religious situation among the Polish immigrants in this country are five in number: (1) Of more and better qualified workers, (2) of a higher grade of religious litera-

ture, (3) of a definite and consistent policy of Polish
evangelization on the part of organized Protestant
forces, (4) of interdenominational co-operation, and
(5) of the relation of the foreign language church
to racial assimilation and national unification.

Workers.—The biggest and hardest problem fac-
ing the religious work among the Poles is that of
workers. The men and women who are to be leaders
in the reconstruction of the Polish religious life
must be men and women of the very finest spiritual
and intellectual qualifications. They must possess
deep religious convictions; a strong faith in the
Gospel of Jesus as the only hope of individual and
social regeneration and in Jesus' ideal of life as the
only Way of life leading to righteousness and justice, achievement and success, peace and happiness;
a single purpose, namely, to serve their fellow-coun-
trymen along the line of religious idealism and
practical Christian helpfulness; an unfaltering devotion and loyalty to that purpose; and undaunted
courage in the prosecution of their great work. The
religious work among the Poles is of such nature
that, unless the workers are blest with these spiritual qualifications, they will not be able to cope with
its problems, difficulties, and discouragements.

Moreover, the Polish workers must have the best
possible mental training and intellectual equipment
for their work. The class of people they have to
deal with is not, as has already been stated, the ignorant, unthinking, credulous class; but the men-
tally wide-awake, thinking, reading, doubting, and
inquiring class. These are the people that are
breaking away from the Catholic Church, and that
are in need of new religious leadership. If they are
to be saved from complete loss of religion and of
its dynamic power and inspiration, they must be ap-
proached by men and women qualified, intellectually and spiritually, to be their leaders. No half-

baked individuals with, maybe, a lot of enthusiasm, but very little knowledge, insight, and understanding can win the confidence of these people, still less help them to rebuild their religious conceptions and life wisely and soundly. It was the well trained Paul, rather than any of the simple, uneducated Galilean fishermen, who helped the religiously disintegrating Gentile world most to a reconstruction of its religion and life on a new and better foundation.

Then, too, the religious workers among the Poles, or any other immigrant group, must have an American point of view. This does not mean that they should lose their feeling of oneness with their people, or their sympathy with Polish historical traditions, ideals, and aspirations. Far from that. Should that ever happen, their usefulness would terminate at once. We can acceptably minister and really lead only when we truly love and identify ourselves fully with those whom we wish to help. The Polish workers must, therefore, be thoroughly identified with the life of their people, and must share their ideals and aspirations sympathetically. At the same time, however, they must be well acquainted with American history, religious, social, and political institutions; they must understand American life in all its phases, its spirit, and its idealism; they must be thoroughly sympathetic with best American traditions and aims in order that they may be able to interpret these to their own people to the end that their people may not forever be strangers in a strange land.

Most of the Polish people are here to stay. By naturalization they have identified themselves with the life of the nation. Their children are growing up into an indistinguishable part of the nation. The parents, too, should be led, through proper acquaintance with American institutions, their spirit, and ideals, to the full enjoyment of their American citizenship as well as to a realization of their responsibility as American citizens. They should contribute of the best in their national history, tradition and character to the development, strength, and power of their adopted country. Their life here can be what it should be only when they feel perfectly at home; and their value to the nation will be in proportion to their entrance into its life. A wise leadership, well acquainted and thoroughly sympathetic with the inherited tradition and the new environment can render a great service to both—the foreign-born citizen and the nation—along the line of mutual understanding and helpfulness. A leadership that still lives and moves and has its being altogether and exclusively in the old environment, is useless in the new, with its new atmosphere and problems.

Now, anyone, at least in a slight measure acquainted with the Protestant work among the Poles, knows well that there is a painful scarcity of Protestant religious workers adequately equipped for their stupendous task. The first special business before the American Protestant Churches, therefore, is to recruit and train a strong well-equipped Polish religious leadership. Unless the Protestant Churches have real leaders, and enough of them, they cannot help the Poles to reconstruct their disintegrating religious life.

Literature.—The second problem in the Polish religious work is that of literature. Polish evangelical religious literature is surprisingly limited in quantity, very poor in qualtiy, and distressingly antiquated—lacking in adaptation to modern religious problems, perplexities, and needs. Polish religious books and pamphlets available in this country number scarcely 100 different copies, and as a matter of fact the writer has been able to get together only

70 different copies. The majority of these are small pamphlets and tracts. Forty per cent. of them are translations from other languages, fifty per cent. are reprints of tracts published abroad, and ten per cent. consist of Seventh Day Adventist propaganda tracts. A very small portion of this literature, if any at all, is adapted to meet either the religious difficulties, or the spiritual yearnings and needs of the average Pole of today, with whom the Protestant Churches have to deal, and whom it is their business to reach and to help.

Polish religious periodical literature suffers the same limitations. Altogether there are three Polish monthly religious periodicals. The "Słowa Żywota," or "Words of Life," published by Rev. Dr. R. J. Miller, of Pittsburgh, Pa., the Chicago Tract Society coöperating, is the oldest. This paper is strictly evangelical and undenominational in character. The tone of its reading matter is devotional rather than instructive; and while it has filled a very important place, it has not made an appeal to the very class of Poles who should be the special concern of American Protestantism. Great credit, however, is due Dr. Miller for his self-sacrifice, patience, and perseverance in carrying on the publication of this paper for over twenty years in the face of financial and editorial difficulties, which have been trying enough to force an average man to give up the thankless enterprise long ago. The next oldest Polish religious monthly is "Źródło Prawdy," "The Source of Truth." This paper is published by the Baptists, represents the Polish Baptist work, and is strongly denominational in character. Its reading matter is, on the whole, good and frequently much to the point. The "Postęp," or "Advance," the publication of which was discontinued with the December number, 1920, was a semi-religious and strictly undenominational monthly, published by the

Presbyterians. Its attempt was to meet the intellectual and spiritual needs of the more thoughtful and critical Poles, the very group that is both most restless and most hopeful. Unfortunately, its publication had to be discontinued, owing to inadequate financial support.

The Polish secular press includes a number of publications that are open to and from time to time publish religious articles. Their difficulty, however, has been to get readable religious matter, dealing with religion in a broad, unbiased, intelligent, and constructive manner. In this connection, it must be confessed that the Protestants have not the men who either are qualified to write such articles, or have the time for writing them. If we had the men with proper qualifications and the necessary time for literary work, the Polish secular press would be more than open to the publication of good religious articles.

It should not be necessary to emphasize the importance of good, up-to-date, constructive Polish religious literature, book and periodical, for use among the Poles at this critical transitional stage in their religious life. Yet the lack of such literature is so acute and so serious that one need not hesitate to call the attention of the Protestant religious forces to it, and urge a proper and speedy remedy. The second imperative task before the Protestant Churches, then, is to provide for (1) the publication of at least one, and if possible two, good, strong, undenominational Polish religious periodicals, which will command the attention and the respect of the more thoughtful Poles, and (2) the preparation and publication of better and more up-to-date Polish tract and book religious literature, namely, (a) *devotional* but instructive; (b) *theological* or *philosophical* but written in simple readable language, dealing with religious fundamentals, solving religious problems that perplex the modern man, and giving the readers an intellectual basis for the reconstruction of their religious life; (c) *historical*, dealing with the development of the Christian Church, the Reformation, and the rise of the different Protestant denominations and their distinguishing characteristics; (d) *sociological*, treating social problems from the standpoint of Christianity, and making the position of the Church clear regarding social justice in industry and commerce, and (e) *a series of Bible-study handbooks* for thoughtful and inquiring adults. Such literature would find great acceptance not only among Polish Protestants, but also among the clergy and laity of the Polish National and the Polish Catholic Churches described above, and among the large number of thoughtful Poles who are at present without any church affiliation; not only among Poles in this country, but also among Poles in the homeland.

Protestant policy.—The question of a definite, consistent, and statesmanlike Protestant policy of aggressive religious work among the Poles constitutes the third problem. Whatever Protestant religious work has heretofore been done among the Poles, it has been largely sporadic and haphazard. A local church, conference, or presbytery has here and there become interested in a local group of Poles, and has tried to minister to them after a fashion in its own way. The national denominational boards have cooperated with the local agencies in these enter prises, wherever they have been asked to, and in as far as expediency has permitted. But they have not had the initiative in the matter, owing to the independence and autonomy of local church bodies. The initiation of new work has, generally speaking, depended on the initiative and aggressiveness of local church organizations. This decentralization of authority and power of initiative has seriously inter-

fered with the development of general definite policies of aggressive religious work among particular
immigrant groups on the part of denominational
boards. The effect of this condition of things has
been very unfavorable to the promotion of religious
work among the Poles, whatever its effect may have
been among other immigrant groups. A difficult
problem cannot be solved by playing at it, but by
taking it seriously and by working on it hard and
systematically; by seeing it whole and by dealing
with it according to a definite plan and in a masterly
way. In order to make the Protestant religious approach to the Poles more effective, the Protestant
forces must, in the third place, develop more definite,
consistent, and more statesmanlike policies for the
prosecution of this work. Weak, incoherent, haphazard efforts will get them nowhere. The work is
very difficult, and its problems are many and intri-
cate.

Interdenominational coöperation.—Closely connected with the problem of the development of more
definite denominational policies for the prosecution
of the religious work among the Poles is that of
inter-denominational coöperation in this work. The
immigrant groups, it must be remembered, are racial, and in some cases, like that of the Poles, also
religious units. They act as units, and must be
dealt with as units, in the first generation at least.
After they have been absorbed into the life of the
nation as integral component parts of it, then we
not only may, but can and must deal with them
as individuals. In the first generation, however, we
must deal with them as groups; for they live and
act in groups. Then, to reach any given immigrant
group effectively, we must have quite an outfit of
absolutely necessary means: workers speaking the
language of the group; literature, tract, book, and
periodical; a hymnology and books of worship with

special forms for special services like baptism, communion, weddings, and funerals, and a number of other more or less important things. These obviously cannot be properly and adequately provided for by individual efforts of this or that local church, group of churches, or even denominations; for no denomination, at present at least, is either willing to confine its missionary effort to one or two particular immigrant groups, or capable to care adequately for them all. In the Polish work, for instance, some denominations report as having one Polish church, some two or three, and only one has more than a dozen Polish churches and missions. No special argument, therefore, is needed to show that under existing circumstances no denomination has or can have the necessary equipment for handling the religious work among the Poles with any degree of efficiency.

Nor is it specially desirable that the Protestant denominations should try to be self-sufficient in every particular. There are some things that can be done by interdenominational coöperation; and they can be done this way better and more economically. Among such interdenominational coöperative enterprises in the Polish work may be included: (1) the recruiting and training of workers, (2) the publication of one or two good religious periodicals, (3) the preparation and publication of Polish religious literature, and (4) the promotion of interdenominational conferences of religious workers for mutual acquaintance, exchange of experiences, encouragement, and inspiration, in order to save these workers from the altogether too common feeling of isolation and loneliness, which frequently drives them to cry with Elijah: "It is enough, O Lord; take me away from this job; for the feeling of being a solitary champion of thy cause is too dreadful; I cannot stand it any longer" (Cf. 1 Kings 19:3, 4,

10). We have come to recognize the importance of interdenominational coöperation along several lines of work on the foreign field, is it too much to ask of ourselves to recognize its importance on the home field?

The foreign-language churches and American national unity.—The fifth problem is that of the relation of the foreign-language church to racial assimilation and national unification. Strictly speaking, this is not a real problem, but chiefly imaginary only. For that reason it should not be discussed here as a problem at all, were it not for the constant fears of some timid patriots that the foreign-language church tends to be an obstacle in the way of racial assimilation and of national unification. To allay the useless fears of these troubled souls and set their minds and hearts at ease as speedily as possible, it must be said at the outset that the foreign-language church in this country is only a temporary, transitional institution, serving the needs of practically only the first generation of immigrants and possibly the older portion of the second generation. Thereafter it of necessity either becomes transformed into an English-speaking church, or quietly passes away with the old order of things. This transformation is going on constantly, steadily, noiselessly, as the growth of all natural things. Feverish uneasiness about it and loss of sleep over it is not going to hasten the change, but it may seriously disturb, hinder, and retard it.

As a caution to the American Protestant Churches carrying on work among immigrants an observation is in order, calling their attention to the altogether too frequent, very loose and incorrect use of descriptive terms. The substitution of "Americanization," or "Christian Americanization," for "evangelization" or "Christianization" is not only a very incorrect use of language, but also very misleading and frequently very mischievous. In the case of the Poles, for instance, who have been made keenly conscious of their nationality as a result of forcible Germanizing and Russianizing policies, and who have been led purposely by the Roman Church to associate these denationalization policies with religious faiths differing from that of the Poles, namely, Russian Orthodoxy and German Protestantism, and to identify Roman Catholicism with their national independence and liberty,—to speak of "Americanization" even if that term is sugarcoated with the adjective "Christian" calls instantly to their minds all their unpleasant experiences under Russian and German rule, stirs up in them all the old fears and resentments, and places them unnecessarily in an antagonistic position to the influences of their new environment, national and religious. The American *laissez faire* policy in matters of nationalism is both wise and sound. Absolute non-interference with inherited national feelings has been the strength of Americanism and a most potent cause in the promotion of American patriotism and of national unity. The foreign-born loves this country and its government and institutions instinctively and passionately, because he is not molested here everlastingly about language and nationality.

It is very doubtful whether the so-called "Christian Americanization" propaganda of the American Protestant Churches is helping to speed up real Americanization of the immigrants; but it is certain that it does interfere with the process of their Christianization. This is particularly true of the religious work among the Poles. The Polish priests have not been slow to use that as a scarecrow to frighten the Poles away from Protestant Churches. Jesus was very careful not to allow himself to be entangled with his Gospel in the meshes of national sentiments and prejudices, it would, therefore, be well for the Christian Church to exercise the same caution, and not to rush where the Master refused to tread. "Render unto Cæsar the things that are Cæsar's, and unto God the things that are God's." Americanization is the business of the State. If the State sees any need of a special Americanization propaganda, it doubtless will attend to it, and look after it. The Church's specific business is Christianization. Let her discharge her specific duty well toward the immigrants; and no foreign-born citizen, really and truly Christianized, will be found wanting in American patriotism and loyalty.

PRACTICAL SOLUTIONS

Problems call for solutions; they become tasks; and the more difficult they are the more imperative is the duty to solve them.

We have discovered that among the special problems in the religious work among the Poles are those of more and better trained workers and of more and better religious literature. The question now is how can we secure both?

There are two ways we may go about getting the necessary workers; (1) we may hope to find them here and there among the children of the Polish immigrants, or (2) we may import them from Poland from among the Protestant students there. On the face of it it would seem that the first method would be preferable. It would give us workers brought up and educated in this country, with an intellectual training equal to our English-speaking ministry and having an American point of view. There are, however, several things against it. First, it is uncertain. We have depended upon it for the last thirty years, and it has not yielded any results. Secondly, it is very slow in its operation. If American in-

dustry had depended on the natural increase of
population for its workers, it would be still in its
infancy, and the country would still be largely an
undeveloped wilderness. Thirdly, it is unpromis-
ing. The American brought-up children of the immigrants have neither the language of their parents,
nor the sympathetic understanding of the first generation immigrant. Workers recruited from the
second generation of Poles in this country, on finishing their education here, would have to be sent
for one or two years to Poland in order to get the
language and a better and more sympathetic understanding of their own people. Unless that were
done, they would be practically useless for work
among their people; nor is it likely that they could
be induced to take it up. The second method, on
its face, is not very appealing. The American
churchman, unlike the American captain of industry,
is very reluctant to think of importing workers; and
his reluctance is based, in certain respects, on some
good reasons. Nevertheless the method has a good
deal to commend it. It eliminates the element of
time and long waiting as well as the expense of
preparation; it is more dependable and more promising as to results than the first method. Some of
our best workers among the Poles in this country
were picked out on the other side, brought to this
country for the specific purpose of doing Christian
work among their countrymen, given the finishing
touches of education in our institutions, were put to
work, and have done excellently well. What has
been done can be done again, provided we have the
vision and the will. The American Protestant
Churches should be as resourceful and as enterprising as American industry. Instead of helplessly
waiting for a chance volunteer here and there, we
should look for volunteers where there is a reasonably good prospect of finding them, among the

Protestant students of Polish gymnasia. This plan would give us a half-finished product. This, in fact, is all that we should look for. We should not look for a completely finished product; for we want to do the finishing of it on this side of the Atlantic. We should try to get young men with an education corresponding to an American-college course, and should make provision to give them the seminary training in this country. This would enable them to acquire the English language, to become acquainted with American conditions and the better side of American life, and to see things from our American point of view. The seminary course would serve the double purpose of a theological training and a process of acclimatization.

The theological training of these young men should be provided for in our regular theological seminaries. They should by no means be segregated either in a Polish department connected with some American seminary, or in a polyglot theological institution, still less in a special Polish theological training school. If they are to become sympathetically acquainted with American life, its spirit and its ideals, they must be placed in an American atmosphere; they must come under the instruction of American professors; and they must have the contact of American students. Educational segregation of any group of students does not promote Americanization, in the best sense of the term, any more than the segregation of immigrants in our city and country communities.

However, it would be very desirable for the men to live together for the purpose of keeping up the language, cultivating their spiritual life together, promoting their common interests, and of developing a sense of unity, an *esprit de corps,* among themselves. To an all-round equipment for their special work this is just as important as keeping in the closest possible touch with American life. They must have both contacts. The loss of either contact is apt to be serious. This arrangement could be easily carried out in a city like Chicago, where several denominations have their own theological seminaries; Presbyterians—McCormick Seminary, Congregationalists—Chicago Theological Seminary affiliated with the University of Chicago, Baptists— the Divinity School of the University, and Methodists—Garrett Biblical Institute at Evanston. Here the Polish students of the various denominations could be brought and grouped together in a Polish Student Guild House, with a superintendent in charge, who would be their counsellor and guide; and their studies they would pursue in their respective denominational schools. This suggestion furnishes a practical as well as an economical solution of a very difficult problem.

This Guild House could hold also a press, and be the center of Polish religious publication activity, where a good interdenominational Polish religious monthly and other Polish religious literature could be issued. The superintendent of the House could act as Editor-in-chief of all Polish publications, and the students could coöperate by furnishing some literary matter, or by helping in the press room, or in various other ways. This is another practical solution of a second very difficult problem.

This suggested solution, however, assumes that the Protestant Churches earnestly desire to deal with the religious situation among the Poles in an aggressive manner; and that along these two lines of recruiting and training workers and of developing an up-to-date Polish religious literature they are willing and ready to coöperate in the interest of the Kingdom.

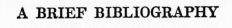

A BRIEF BIBLIOGRAPHY

A BRIEF BIBLIOGRAPHY

BAIN, R. N. *Slavonic Europe*, Cambridge University Press, 1908.

BAIN, R. N., *The Last King of Poland*, G. P. Putnam's Sons, N. Y., 1909.

BALCH, EMILY G., *Our Slavic Fellow-Citizens*, Charities Publishing Committee, N. Y., 1910.

BENSON, E. F., *The White Eagle of Poland*, George H. Doran Company, N. Y., 1919.

BOSWELL, A. B., *Poland and the Poles*, Dodd, Mead & Co., N. Y., 1919.

BRANDES, GEORGE, *Poland, a Study of the Land, People and Literature.*

CHOLONIEWSKI, ANTONI, *The Spirit of Polish History*, Polish Book Importing Co., N. Y., 1908.

CLARK, E. F., *Old Homes of New Americans*, (Chaps. 4-6), Houghton, Mifflin & Co., Boston, 1913.

GARDNER, MONICA, *Poland*, Charles Scribner's Sons, N. Y., 1919.

GIBBONS, H. A., *The Reconstruction of Poland*, The Century Co., N. Y., 1917.

HARLEY, J. H., *Poland—Past and Present*, Allen & Unwin, Ltd., London, 1917.

HAYDEN, JOEL B., *Religious Work among the Poles in America*, Missionary Education Movement, N. Y., 1916.

HOURWICH, I. A., Ph. D., *Immigration and Labor*, G. P. Putnam's Sons, N. Y., 1912.

JENKS AND LAUCK, *Immigration*, Funk & Wagnalls Co., N. Y., 1912.

LEWINSKI-CORWIN, E. H., Ph. D., *The Political History of Poland*, Polish Book Importing Co., N. Y., 1917.

LITTLE, F. D., *Sketches in Poland*, Frederick A. Stokes Co., N. Y., 1914.

LORD, R. H., Ph. D., *The Second Partition of Poland*, Harvard University Press, Cambridge, Mass., 1915.

McCLURE, ARCHIBALD, *Leadership of the New America*, George H. Doran Company, N. Y., 1916.

MORFILL, W. R., *Poland*, G. P. Putnam's Sons, N. Y., 1893.

PHILLIPS, W. A., *Poland*, Henry Holt & Co., N. Y.

Poland, Her People, History, Finance, Science, Literature, Art and Social Development, Petite Encyc. Polonaise (Eng. Edition), Herbert Jenkins, Ltd., London, 1919.

RADOSAVLJEVICH, PAUL R., Ph. D., *Who Are the Slavs?* 2 vols. Richard G. Badger, Boston, 1919.

SHRIVER, WILLIAM P., D. D., *Immigration Forces*, Missionary Education Movement, N. Y., 1913.

SLOCOMBE, G. E., *Slavonic Europe*, Cambridge University Press, 1905.

VAN NORMAN, L. E., *Poland, the Knight among Nations*, Fleming H. Revell Co., N. Y., 1908.

THOMAS AND ZNANIECKI, *Polish Peasants in Europe and America*, 5 vols., University of Chicago Press, 1916.

WHITTON, T. E., *A History of Poland from Earliest Times*, Constable & Co., Ltd., London, 1917.

WINTER, N. O., *Poland of Today and Yesterday*, L. C. Page & Co., Boston, 1913.

ALMY, FREDERICK, *Huddled Poles of Buffalo*, The Survey, Feb. 14th, 1911.

COULTER, C. W., *Poles of Cleveland*, Cleveland Americanization Committee, 1919.

DANIELS, J., *Americanizing 80,000 Poles*, The Survey, June 4, 1919.

GARRETT, L. B., *Notes on the Poles in Buffalo*, The Survey, Dec. 5th, 1904.

Jan, the Polish Minor, The Outlook, March 26, 1910.
Journal of the American-Polish Chamber of Commerce and Industry, 953 Third Ave., New York City.
Spirit of Poles in America, The Survey, Sept. 28, 1918.
The Pole in the Land of the Puritan, New England Magazine, October, 1903.

INDEX